CHANGE:
THREAT OR OPPORTUNITY
FOR HUMAN PROGRESS?

DEDICATION

The five volumes in this series, the product of a
collaborative international effort, are dedicated to
all those global citizens committed to serving
human progress to the best of their abilities.

CHANGE:
THREAT OR OPPORTUNITY
FOR HUMAN PROGRESS?

Edited by
Üner Kirdar

VOLUME III

GLOBALIZATION
OF MARKETS

United Nations
New York
1992

The contents of this book do not necessarily reflect
the views of the United Nations or of the United Nations Development
Programme. The papers in this volume were contributed by authors in
their personal capacities and they are solely responsible for their views.
Authors are listed with their affiliations at the time of the
Antalya Round Table.

United Nations Publications
United Nations
Room DC2-853
New York, N.Y. 10017, U.S.A.

United Nations Publications
Palais des Nations
1221 Geneva 10
Switzerland

Vol. III: Globalization of Markets
U.N. Sales No. E.91.III.B.7
ISBN 92-1-126026-4

Complete Set (Vol. I–Vol. V):
U.N. Sales No. E.91.III.B.10
ISBN 92-1-126029-9

CONTENTS

Chapter 1

ISSUES
AND QUESTIONS

Üner Kirdar

A revolutionary change is currently taking place in the world's financial and securities markets. The deregulation process taking effect through the opening up of national financial markets to international competition and the abolition of exchange controls and other restrictions are now worldwide phenomena. Thus, the traditional division between national and international policy-making in financial, monetary and securities issues is becoming obsolete. The national origin of firms is losing importance—indeed, it is anachronistic. Success depends increasingly on the relative financial strength, competitiveness, skills and efficiency of individual firms, regardless of the country of origin. Different types of investment firms and commercial banks, full-service brokers, dealers, asset managers, insurance companies, central banks, supranationals, all are taking an active part in these markets. They are providing new financial products and services worldwide and are offering more investment opportunities and greater flexibility, at a lower cost than ever before.

It can therefore be asserted that financial and security markets are today becoming globalized, at least in the financial sense. At present, it is no longer trade but the transnational movement of capital which is the main driving force of the world economy. As a result of new technology, informatics and communications facilities, which permit worldwide transactions within 24 hours, financial exchanges are outweighing trade as the major source of international capital movements, in a ratio of 20 to 1. They are also determining world monetary exchange rates. Foreign financial exchange transactions alone are reaching approximately $350 billion a day. According to a reliable estimate, in 1988 alone a staggering amount of more than $10 trillion worth of securitized funds moved across national frontiers.

In sum, each day, the powerful role of the corporate world in the globalization and channelling of capital in the world economy is becoming more apparent. Similarly, the worldwide maintenance of orderly and stable exchange rates and multilateral systems of payments between different countries is no longer regulated by the International Monetary Fund (IMF), as envisaged after the post-war period. They are, in fact, primarily determined through the market forces generated by private financial institutions, in world currency and stock markets. In this context, it should be noted that the only international regulatory mechanism in existence at present is the Basel Committee, which is limited to transnational activities of commercial banks. As became more apparent after the stock market crash of October 1987, there is no similar mechanism to review the regulation of non-banking institutions on an international basis.

Changes in the monetary system

In the aftermath of the Second World War, the IMF was designed primarily to foster global macroeconomic conditions conducive to the growth of all nations; help countries to promote exchange stability; maintain orderly exchange arrangements; avoid competitive exchange depreciation; monitor world economic trends and international macroeconomic policies; facilitate the expansion and balanced growth of international trade, and contribute thereby to the promotion and maintenance of high levels of employment, real income and the development of the productive resources of all countries.

None the less, over the past two decades, the major industrialized countries have succeeded in escaping from IMF policy monitoring. Instead of using their IMF drawing rights, they have chosen to utilize capital market resources, thus avoiding IMF policy prescriptions and adjustment conditionalities. In the 1980s, the Fund's credits, advice and policy subscriptions were limited to developing countries. Major industrial powers have chosen to regulate their financial matters according to their own national policy decisions and, whenever required, through consultations restricted to themselves.

Two radical changes in the world's monetary system created at Bretton Woods in 1944 have led to a serious weakening of global cooperation between Governments in the monetary and financial areas. These changes are: the breakdown of the par value exchange rate systems in the early 1970s, during the first oil crisis, and the tacit agreement among the governments of the major industrialized countries to let their exchange rates float; and the explosive growth of international capital markets through financial exchanges and private lendings of investment and commercial banks. These developments have also undercut the main rationale for the creation and allocation of new special drawing rights resources.

Today's global capital flows and international trade far exceed what was anticipated by the founders of the Bretton Woods institutions. However, the dynamism and globalization of capital and security markets have brought with them new problems, evident today in large global imbalances, excessive volatility in the exchange rates of currencies and unsustainable levels of indebtedness.

With the end of United States supremacy in the world economy, the world monetary system ceased to rely solely on the United States dollar as the international reserve currency. The dollar had been losing its central role since Washington closed the gold window in 1971. Since then, other currencies have shared the international role that formerly belonged to the dollar. But the present "non-system" has evolved without design and with no agreement that the currencies would be defended as unconditional international liquidity assets.

As the world monetary system fragments into regional blocs, the ad hoc currency system also fragments. According to some views, a new world monetary system, once again based on gold, may ultimately emerge as an option. Thus, in the event of a world currency reform, the restoration of the status of gold as an international reserve currency cannot be ruled out.

Questions

These revolutionary and fundamental changes bring a rewarding dynamism to the markets, but they also raise the following important policy questions, which have yet to be answered.

Are the financial and security markets at present globalized in the true sense? Do all countries—especially developing countries, which have the majority of the world's population but little economic power—play a role in the so-called globalized financial markets, or are some only marginalized actors in this staggering world of economic and financial growth?

What are the strengths and weaknesses of current global market mechanisms? Does an effective supervisory structure exist to oversee transactions of the financial markets? What role do Governments play at present and what role should they play in the future in this area? Is there sufficient regulatory coordination and information-sharing among Governments in this area? Is there not a need to develop an international framework to define the basic purpose of and need for the well-coordinated global regulation of financial institutions to ensure some type of harmonization among institutions participating in global financial markets?

Should there be an initiative to harmonize regulations either among different types of institutions or among countries? If the answer is affirmative, what types of harmonization among institutions and countries would be desirable, especially taking into account recent and potential changes in technology affecting financial markets and the trend towards globalization of markets and institutions? Should the harmonization of regulations cover such issues as national structural differences between the financial institutions, their relationships to their own Government, taxation and accounting areas?

Today, besides foreign exchange, Government-issued debts comprise the most globally traded category of securities in all major capital markets. Does the present prevailing international debt crisis that is seriously affecting the world economy and the well-being of billions of people living in more than 70 countries indicate a need for global cooperation concerning the role of the markets or institutions?

What measures are needed to re-establish and strengthen the surveillance functions of international mechanisms so that worldwide economic growth with orderly trade, monetary and financial exchanges can be resumed and stimulated? Is it possible to establish a system of accountability and coordination of macroeconomic national policies in order to ensure their compatibility with the objectives of global development?

Is there not a strong need to give the IMF a new mandate to toughen its surveillance over the national economic and monetary policies of key countries?

If there is no mutual surveillance of and coordination among the monetary, fiscal and economic policies of key industrialized countries, how can the reasonable stability of exchange rates, prices, rates of growth and the management of the global economy be maintained?

What are the measures needed to ensure that the IMF plays its original role in the determination of exchange rates around which currency stabilization efforts are undertaken?

Could gold once again become the central international reserve currency?

Chapter 2

GLOBALIZATION OF FINANCIAL MARKETS AND THE MONETARY SYSTEM

Osama J. Faquih*

The ongoing process of global integration which has now become a world phenomenon means, basically, a general opening up of domestic financial markets to international competition. It has brought about great changes, high expectations and risks to the international financial arena. The end result is not yet known, but it is already clear that the process is one of integration and not unification, for there will always remain differences in character and scope between the various financial markets. Some markets are likely to emerge and grow in the process, while others may remain excluded or may simply be forced to fade away. After all, the global market thrives on these differences, which stem naturally from different strategies, assumptions and expectations with regard to growth rates, exchange rates, inflation levels, perceived risks and differences in market rules and regulations.

The origins of the globalization process date back to as early as the 1960s with the development of the Eurocurrency and the Eurobond markets. The acceleration of the process has reflected the interaction of a number of wide-ranging factors and circumstances which may be summarized as follows.

*Director-General and Chairman of the Board, Arab Monetary Fund, Abu Dhabi.

The end of the Bretton Woods system and the move of the major currencies to a free-floating exchange regime reduced pressure on the major economies to do their share in maintaining equilibrium in the international payments system. Thus, huge surpluses and deficits in fiscal and external trade balances were built and persisted, and these, in turn, fueled the growth of international capital seeking investment opportunities. The drastic adjustments in the prices of some of the major internationally traded commodities contributed to the sizeable growth of international capital and triggered a general rush for the recycling process. The ongoing deregulation of financial markets and the easing of exchange controls gave international capital increased mobility between markets. The growth of universal banking blurred demarcation lines between various financial sectors, further increasing capital mobility.

Financial innovations, such as swaps, portfolio insurance and forward markets, helped increase substitutability of investment assets and allowed for the mitigation of the risk involved in these assets, thereby enlarging the stock of acceptable investment instruments and adding depth to the international financial market. Similarly, the drive towards securitization of various obligations allowed financial institutions to shift risks to ultimate investors and increased their ability to handle a much larger volume of transactions, develop new products and secure economies of scale.

Finally, the remarkable advance in communications technology allowed for speedy and safe transmission of information among the various operators and gave them the ability to operate in various markets concomitantly and to transact in huge volumes at reduced cost.

The general impact of the globalization process on the financial industry itself and its regulatory environment and on financial and macroeconomic policy at large has been far-reaching. Competition has increased sharply among banks and between bank and non-bank financial institutions. The industry is witnessing a progressive move towards conglomeration, and size and scale are becoming much more important for the provision of a multitude of products and services.

With globalization, the regulatory environment has become one of deregulation with regard to areas which have an impact on competitiveness, and of more regulation in those areas which are related to prudence and risk control. On the one hand, the traditional separation of the structure of the financial industry into four separate sectors—commercial banking, investment banking, securities trading, and insurance—has been all but either eliminated (in the United Kingdom and Canada) or continuously eroded (as is happening in Japan and the United States). On the other hand, the losses incurred in a number of countries as a result of problems faced by some international banks, and the failure of some institutions during the mid-1970s, have led to the recognition of new types of risks and generated a new approach to regulation for fear that foreign branches and subsidiaries may escape supervision altogether. This has led to increased coordination among central banking authorities of major economies to streamline the regulatory environment. The work of the Cooke Committee and, later, the Basel Committee is particularly familiar with regard to the globalization of commercial banking regulations.

In the new global environment, cooperation has also become a necessity at the level of macroeconomic policy. The policy maker is no longer independent, as is illustrated by the frequency and scope of talks at the various meetings of the group of major industrialized countries.

In a world of free exchange controls and floating exchange rates, the central banker can no longer unilaterally tighten credit, thus producing higher interest rates, without triggering capital inflow to the home country to take advantage of the higher yield. The increase in demand for one's own currency would soon be reflected in a higher exchange rate, which would in turn stimulate imports over exports, thereby affecting external trade balances. Trade partners may counter either by taking advantage of the new market conditions to improve their terms of trade *vis-à-vis* the concerned country, or be more concerned with the capital outflow towards it and end up raising their own interest rates, although they may not need to do this for strictly domestic economic reasons. In other words, globalization increases interdependence, and adjustment in the global market is done more and more through the price mechanism of exchange rates and interest rates.

Role for developing countries

It goes without saying that developing countries have so far been at the losing end of the global market adjustment process. What role is there, if any, for these countries in the global financial market?

First, they lack the means and the appropriate degree of policy sophistication necessary to benefit from the global market mechanism. These weaknesses are clearly reflected in the direction of international capital flows which, during the past few years, has been almost a one-way street from them to the industrialized countries. To slow the financial drain caused by capital flight, most developing countries are forced to adopt policies, such as high interest rates, which are in direct conflict with their investment and development objectives.

Secondly, developing countries, which have the majority of the world's population but little economic power, are unequal partners with the industrial world in the coordination dialogue associated with the new global market environment. In some cases, they find themselves completely sidelined, as has happened with the work of the Cooke and Basel committees. Developing countries' banks are finding it necessary to accept the requirements of these committees for commercial banking regulations in order to operate in the global financial market. The implications are of great concern and deserve a closer look before we can draw the right lessons and make the proper policy recommendations.

Role of the markets

What are the implications of net capital inflows to developing economies? What role could the global market and institutions play to help solve the debt crisis?

The lessons we may derive in this regard from the situation of member countries of the Arab Monetary Fund (AMF) could in many aspects be easily extrapolated to the rest of the developing world. One such aspect of importance is the existence of so-called deficit countries and so-called surplus countries. The availability of surplus capital goes hand in hand with the degree of openness of domestic financial markets and henceforth its sensitivity to the impact of globalization.

Surplus economies, which are mainly those of the oil-exporting countries of the Gulf, are open economies in the sense that there are no exchange restrictions or other controls on capital flows. Although not totally integrated with the world financial market, these economies receive the full impact of international financial developments but have yet to develop the monetary and fiscal policy instruments necessary for survival in the highly competitive and more sophisticated global market environment.

Moreover, the limited absorptive capacity at home, the lack of depth of local markets and the increasing sophistication of private investors accentuates the sensitivity of these economies to exchange rate fluctuations and interest rate adjustments in the global market. The monetary authorities have tried to minimize the exchange rate effects by lining up their currencies more or less with the United States dollar, which is the major currency for the payments settlements of these countries. But the reduction of investment risks in dollar-denominated instruments that this entails has facilitated capital outflows in recent years. To discourage this outflow, authorities are forced to keep domestic interest rates close to United States dollar rates, which are not necessarily at levels resulting from domestic economic considerations.

On the one hand, reciprocity requirements of the global system are progressively eroding the semi-control that domestic banks have been enjoying in the home market in recent years; on the other hand, in order to operate abroad and compete in the international market, these banks face strong competition from bigger and more sophisticated financial establishments, as well as pressure by outside regulatory agencies which subject them to different risk standards.

On the positive side, domestic banks are improving their skills, upgrading their operations and services, improving their information disclosure and adopting improved accounting systems and procedures, although they still lag behind in these last two areas. For most banks in the surplus countries of the Gulf, capital adequacy is not an issue at present; it is easily in line with the new international regulatory requirements of 8 per cent.

With regard to the banking sector of the so-called deficit economies, which represent about two thirds of AMF membership, the globalization challenge has been even greater. These countries are generally characterized by a shortage of domestic funds necessary to finance investment and development projects. Most are forced to adopt exchange restrictions to control capital flight.

In the absence of a sophisticated financial system, the role of the banking sector is of fundamental importance to these Arab developing economies. By providing strong support for both banks and their deposit holders, Governments have acted to promote the banking system as a source of both short-term credit and long-term finance. Central banks provide rediscount facilities to assure the banks a degree of liquidity in the event of major deposit withdrawals. To prevent banking crises, bailouts tend to be arranged for commercial banks in financial difficulties rather than risking the consequences of a run on these banks.

For lack of deposit insurance, repayment of the principal of small deposits is guaranteed by the Government, and most major banks are, in fact, fully or partially owned by the public sector.

But the introduction of the Basel standard, which underlines the need for banks to be free-standing institutions in their own right, presents a major challenge for the banking sector of these developing countries. Providing all the public-sector banks with sufficient capital is beyond their means. Domestic resources are not sufficient to raise the necessary fresh capital to reach the Basel Committee's 8 per cent target ratio; external resources are mostly out of the question, as these countries have difficulty even coping with the servicing of past debts. Almost inevitably, the banking sector will remain undercapitalized, and foreign banks will concentrate their business flows through even fewer channels.

The debt problem, which is crippling the financial structures of these economies, is, in fact, intimately related to the inconsistencies of the international financial system. It is mainly the outcome of an overall strong credit expansion by international banks during the 1970s. The expansion was based on expectations that were not realized, and it came to an abrupt halt in August 1982 with the crisis in Mexico, followed by other Latin American countries which announced that they could not meet their scheduled payments without receiving new loans. International commercial banks, which hold around 60 per cent of the total debt of developing countries—expected to exceed $1.3 trillion by the end of 1990—are reluctant to provide new money and cautious in doing so. Hence, financing gaps increased for the AMF debtor countries, as they have for many developing countries, and for nearly six years repayments have exceeded new loans for most of them.

So far, the various plans proposed to solve the problem have been based on the assumption that developing countries should succeed in gradually growing out of their debts. But, in spite of the structural and policy reforms adopted by many of these countries, economic growth has been negatively affected by their limited export potential, unfavourable terms of trade, unstable exchange rates and high interest rates. Financial markets have developed various techniques to help reduce the impact of the debt problem on international banks, which have, in a sense, grown out of the problem by strengthening their capital base, making adequate provisions and marking down the book value of their debt exposure.

Now that there is tacit admission in international financial circles of the need for debt reduction, the international global market ought to use its ingenuity to alleviate the debt burden on developing countries. Various techniques, such as debt-equity swaps, cash buy-backs, securitization of debt and the development of a secondary market to trade it, and the conversion of debt into other assets at discounted prices, are necessary to clear the way for the most heavily indebted countries to reform and restructure their economies.

The global system and developing countries

Is the global system concept conducive to the development of an efficient and balanced domestic financial system in developing economies?

What impact would deregulation have on their securities markets in particular?

While securities markets cannot do much about unrooting the many problems that have caused the debt crisis, it is becoming increasingly clear to developing countries that the strengthening of domestic equity and bond markets could help attract financial resources through direct foreign portfolio investment and could play an important role in solving the crisis. The key public-policy objectives of capital market development in our area are similar to those of many market-oriented economies—namely, mobilization of savings through equity and long-term debt instruments, efficient allocation of those savings into productive investment opportunities in both the public and private sector, access to capital funds by newer businesses and broadening of the ownership base of enterprises through wide distribution of equity shares.

Securities markets, together with banking systems, constitute an important alternative channel of finance in an overall financial market; these two distinct channels can be either competitive, and therefore substituting for one another, or complementary. Substitution is limited primarily to the market for debt finance, but with appropriate government support and subsidization, banks in our region, as well as in other developing countries, have been able to provide long-term debt financing on less costly terms than a bond market would provide. This has contributed to shifting business financing preferences in favour of debt financing over equity financing and has resulted in a less secure pattern of corporate finance and a less efficient allocation of resources. Even in countries in which most long-term finance is channelled through the securities markets, banks may act as securities market institutions providing broker-dealer, trust and investment management services along with standard banking services.

This leads to a key question faced by most developing countries when it comes to defining the right strategy for the development of a healthy and efficient financial market. The question relates to the role that banks should play in the conduct of securities market activity and what policies should be adopted by Governments to influence or even define such relationships. In other words, should government in a developing country with an emerging financial market promote a global market mechanism in which banks operate as securities market institutions or fiduciaries in such a market, or would it be healthier for securities market institutions to remain independent and thus separate from banks.

Proponents of the multi-bank or universal system concept argue that the existing extensive branch bank network allows for economies of scale and more efficient distribution of securities. Opponents point out the unhealthy concentration of economic power that this leads to, the lack of specialization and entrepreneurship, and the negative effects associated with conflicts of interest. Banks as underwriters or brokers may be tempted to encourage their borrowing customers to use the financing method that is most convenient for the bank at the time rather than to use the one that may be most beneficial for the borrower. As portfolio managers, banks may also be tempted to orient trust account purchases to gain equity interests which best serve their banking business and not necessarily the best interest of their clients.

It is the AMF's view that government policy for the development of securities markets should depend largely upon how real the conflicts of interest associated with banks are and how significant are the economies of scale. Perhaps at an early stage of financial development, the active role of banks in the securities market is both desirable and unavoidable. At a later stage of financial market development, however, empirical evidence has shown that the economies of semi-industrialized developing countries tend to be more efficient and better served with a wide variety of liquid instruments, with more diverse risk/reward opportunities for savers, borrowers and investors alike, when there is mainly specialization of function and a high degree of competition between and among securities market firms, on the one hand, and banking institutions, on the other, than in those countries where banking entities tend to dominate the securities markets.

Indeed, many developing countries, including AMF member States, have in recent years passed legislation which emphasizes the development and promotion of strong, independent equity markets. Policies are being adopted to eliminate interlocking between major corporate and bank interests and its impact on the solvency and efficiency of the financial system. Some countries have established capital market authorities or securities commissions to implement these policies and regulate market activity.

At the outset, it is important to note that the deregulation movement taking shape in the industrial world has naturally grown out of an institutional structure which has already reached a high degree of competitiveness both in terms of specialization and number of banks and securities firms. Most developing countries, including AMF member States, still have a long way to go to reach that stage.

Conclusions

It is clear that globalization has made developing countries with open economies, such as those of the Gulf, less insulated and has subjected them to disturbances and shocks which are not necessarily a result of domestic factors. The short-run impact has been negative in that sense. But if the countries concerned succeed in adjusting to the new international standards, develop a more formally regulated financial infrastructure and adopt more sophisticated policy tools necessary to counter domestic as well as external disturbances, then globalization might result, in the long run, in a healthier financial industry; this augurs well for the economic development of the region at large.

Industrialized countries should be more responsive to the aspirations of these developing countries. A more sincere and cooperative dialogue should be established to help reduce the negative effects that the new global financial market conditions entail.

Even more urgently, the various techniques of the global market (securitization, buy-backs, debt-equity swaps and conversions of debt), as well as other bilateral mechanisms, ought to be applied more diligently to solve the debt problem. This would allow the indebted countries to reform and restructure their economies. It would lead to a guaranteed flow of repayments, which is to the ultimate benefit of the creditors themselves; would serve as a basis for securing a continuing commitment to sound policies over the medium-term for all concerned parties; and would prepare the ground for making funds available to help debtors adopt the necessary policy reforms to "grow out" of their debts.

The recent experience in both country and corporate over-indebtedness in the Arab region, as well as throughout the developing world, has demonstrated the serious problems that arise from the lack of efficient securities markets to match the highly integrated inter-national banking market. The easier access to bank lending and more difficult access to securities markets led inevitably to a sharp increase in floating-rate debts relative to equity, a combination that historically proved to be unstable, particularly now that major currency risks are involved. In this context, it is the AMF's belief that commercial banks in developing countries ought to concentrate more on their conven-tional role as providers of working capital and trade finance. Securities markets ought to take the major responsibility for providing long-term development finance.

The AMF was honoured to be asked by its member countries to assist in the process of developing their financial markets. Policy deci-sions in some countries are currently being taken to replace informal domestic markets with more operationally efficient formal markets. In these countries, as well as in those where formal markets exist, efforts should be further strengthened to develop financial institutions for underwriting, distributing and market-making in securities, increasing the supply of equities to create more market liquidity, encouraging the flow of savings into equities through supply and demand incentives, and introducing reasonable standards of investor protection, including adequate accounting standards and rules on financial disclosure.

Financial intermediation between Arab countries continues to be largely effected through the international financial centres. The major factor limiting inter-Arab financial intermediation is the prevailing im-balance between the demand for, and supply of, capital at varying maturity levels. Demand for capital in the deficit economies is mostly for project investment needs, which are of a long-term nature and produce low rates of return in the early stage of development. In contrast, supply of capital in the surplus economies is attracted by the liquidity and high interest rate levels of short-term financial instruments provided by the international financial market. Insufficient economic integration between Arab economies is a further limiting factor to inter-Arab financial flows. While efforts are being made through inter-Arab ventures to develop interaction and integration between Arab economies, coordination efforts ought to be further strengthened to develop local capital markets, improve the business and investment environment, help bridge the existing gap between supply and demand and bring about a more reasonable financial equilibrium in the Arab region.

In accordance with its Articles of Agreement, the AMF is in the process of developing a meaningful presence in the international financial markets. It is promoting monetary, financial and economic cooperation among its member States and is progressively playing the role of a banker of its members' central banks. Types of cooperation may be extended in the near future to include the acceptance and administration of their deposits, the management and investment of their reserves and the provision of temporary liquidity in the form of swap arrangements. Furthermore, the AMF intends to enhance its expertise and provide the necessary financial advisory services for the creation of an integrated regional financial centre, as well as to broaden the scope of existing local markets to cover the equities of other member countries and progressively to become active players in the global international financial market.

Chapter 3

IMPLICATIONS FOR THE DEVELOPING WORLD OF THE GLOBALIZATION OF FINANCIAL MARKETS

Nemir Kirdar*

It is obvious that developing countries need to have access to external savings, as well as domestic savings, and it may well be asked whether the revolutionary changes now taking place in the world's financial system can and will work to the benefit of developing countries. Thus, in this paper I would like to describe some of the recent developments in that system and the implications they may have for the world economy.

Sweeping changes

In recent years, financial markets have undergone a sweeping change worldwide. Ever since the Euromarkets emerged 30 years ago, there has been an erosion of the barriers that used to segment currencies and countries or otherwise differentiate financial and non-financial institutions by product, function and geographic market. The trend towards internationalization of financial markets speeded up in the 1980s, stimulating—indeed, if not forcing—the global management of portfolios. Borrowers, whether persons or companies, are no longer confined to

*President and Chief Executive Officer, Arabian Investment Banking Corporation, Manama.

domestic markets or institutions but can seek loans from institutions based abroad and raise equity and debt capital in non-domestic security markets. New financial products have been created to meet investor needs, and competition between financial institutions to provide such products has produced radical structural changes in the financial services industry.

Commercial banks have been particularly affected by these pressures, owing to the erosion of their traditional markets and franchise. The 1980s was marked by the debt crisis of the least developed countries and by a general deflation of shipping, real estate, agriculture, energy and other sectors which were staples of commercial bank business. Bank intermediation costs were raised by capital adequacy and reserve requirements not faced by other financial institutions. As a result, major industrial borrowers drastically reduced their reliance on direct bank financing, relying more on the commercial paper market and on bond issuance to meet their financial needs. The commercial banks did not, of course, remain immobile in the face of these pressures. Where possible, they have securitized assets, selling them off to non-bank financial institutions, and they have moved towards expanding their fee-based services and off-balance-sheet activities. Moreover, particularly in countries where local regulations prohibited banks from security business at home, banks have targeted internationalization of their business, thus further spurring the development of world financial markets.

The forces that have produced this trend towards the globalization or internationalization of financial markets have been important and various. Not least of these was the macroeconomic environment in which financial institutions operated. A great spur to the development of innovatory products was the increasing volatility of interest rates and exchange rates which followed the breakdown of the Bretton Woods fixed exchange rate system and the later adoption of monetary targeting, particularly in the United States. Borrowers and investors sought protection from exchange rate and interest rate risk, and this was soon offered by innovative products such as interest and currency swaps. Whereas in the past, differences in, for example, taxes, regulations, information and preferences tended to produce major discrepancies between interest rates on assets of comparable risk but different currency denomination, today this is not the case. The existence of relatively small swap gains suggests a high degree of integration of world capital markets.

The evolution of international macroeconomic imbalances was also an important factor underlying international capital flows. The escalation of oil prices in the mid-1970s and early 1980s placed substantial financial surpluses in the hands of oil producers. These were intermediated back to the deficit oil-consuming countries largely through the commercial banks, which offered the liquid assets demanded by the surplus oil-producing countries, on the basis of which loans were made to deficit countries. The macroeconomic imbalance changed in the 1980s, with the United States becoming the major deficit country and Japan becoming the major surplus country. Whereas the big international banks provided the most important conduit for channelling international capital flows in the 1970s, the channel of intermediation now became the international security markets, as the United States financed its deficit budget and trade deficits by issuing United States Government securities. The debt problem of the developing countries brought international bank lending virtually to an end.

Two other forces have spurred the growth of global markets. Technological advances in data-processing and communications have cut transaction costs dramatically. Low-cost, instantaneous communications are vital in bringing together financial participants worldwide; they now make possible 24-hour trading.

Finally, the deregulation of domestic financial markets has played a major role. Regulators have allowed new products to emerge in their domestic markets. Controls on cross-bolder capital movements have been relaxed and in many cases have either been eliminated or are in the process of being eliminated. The decision of the European Community to end all restrictions and to create an open market in financial services by 1992 is of major importance. Japan, too, has gone a long way towards the liberalization of Euroyen markets. The United Kingdom was very early in abolishing control over capital movements, and the United States has progressively removed controls that were introduced in the 1960s, although full liberalization of the United States domestic financial market still has some way to go. The United States itself, of course, has benefited greatly from freedom of capital movements in being able to finance its budget and trade deficits at relatively moderate interest rates.

Many Governments are actively promoting their home markets as international financial centres, very often to ensure that financial business remains at home.

Implications of change

Global financial change has both positive and negative implications. The positive ones are easy to see. Competition and better technology have reduced transaction costs, to the benefit of borrowers and lenders. Small depositors increasingly earn market interest rates and have access to a wide array of financial services. Internationalization allows investors to diversify portfolios and allows borrowers to tap markets, to a degree unheard of even 10 years ago. New products enable risks to be separated and have lowered the cost of hedging inflation, interest and exchange rate risks. Reduction of risk encourages investors to save more and invest more. Perhaps most important, efficient international markets tend to equalize returns on investments of comparable risk and, indeed, to allocate capital to where its return is highest, thus raising world output potential.

None the less, there are some possible dangers that have to be guarded against. Some economists have warned that deregulation and financial innovation have encouraged excessive borrowing, by Governments as well as by individuals. Others have argued that the stability of the financial system is placed at risk—first, by the decline in the profitability and quality of the bank loan market, which is forcing undesirable contraction of the traditional, conservative banking sector; secondly, by possible illiquidity in the securities market at a time of crisis; and thirdly, by the lack of transparency in long and complex chains of bank and non-bank participants engaged in particular deals, which makes the monitoring of financial exposure by the monetary authorities very difficult. What is certainly true is that when financial markets are brought closer together, either geographically or in terms of products, economic or financial shocks of one kind or another are more quickly and more widely transmitted from one to another. Domestic markets can be less easily protected or insulated against shocks emanating from other markets abroad. Markets in some products cannot be separated from markets in others, and defaults can spread from one to another. Of course, central banks and the financial institutions themselves recognize these dangers and have taken, or are taking, steps to build up the capital resources of institutions engaged in vulnerable business. Naturally, this has to be done in a manner which is fair internationally and fair between different institutions.

There is one other important implication of the globalization or internationalization of financial markets, namely, the consequences for macroeconomic policies, in particular, monetary policy. Because deregulation and innovation facilitate substitution between domestic assets, while internationalization increases substitution between assets in different currencies, the *modus operandi* of monetary policy is significantly affected. Money itself becomes difficult to define, let alone measure, so that monetary targeting can become a hit-or-miss affair. Moreover, the more integrated that markets become, the more difficult it becomes for countries to pursue independent monetary policies and, therefore, the more important it becomes for the main industrial countries, whose economic stability and performance for the rest of the world is vital, to cooperate internationally in the setting and implementation of policy targets, particularly in ensuring price stability. The globalization of the financial system offers considerable benefits to the world as a whole, but the realization of these benefits depends crucially on the success of Governments in achieving policy coordination.

Developing countries

Let us now turn to the question: will the globalization of financial markets, which I have just described, work to the benefit of developing countries or to their disadvantage? In approaching this issue, we must bear in mind that the more globalized that markets become and the more perfect they become, the more likely it is that capital will be directed to uses and areas throughout the world where the return on it is highest and the risks are lowest, or at least adequately rewarded. This means that if developing countries are to have access to capital through these markets, their economies have to be run in such a manner that the risk-adjusted returns provided to the international investor are competitive with the returns generated elsewhere, a challenging task for the governments of the poorer, less-developed countries of the world.

The less-developed nations of the world need funds now more than ever, and it is certainly in the interest of the industrialized community to aid these nations in their development. In the past, with possibly a few exceptions, developing countries have raised only negligible amounts of capital in world security markets. Commercial bank lending provided a major source of external finance in the 1970s, particularly to the middle-income developing countries, but, as we now know, this form of lending has left behind an intractable debt problem which is inhibiting further private capital flows to the developing world.

In order to put the question into perspective, it might be interesting to observe the following comparison: within the past half century, the total amount of external funds extended to all the developing countries is about $1.2 trillion. In contrast, according to a West German estimate, East Germany would need investments amounting to $600 billion over the period of the 1990s for upgrading its standard of living; in other words, within a decade, a population of 17 million in East Germany would obtain 50 per cent of what was lent to 4 billion people in the developing world over the past 50 years. Furthermore, the funds intended for East Germany are earmarked as investments whereas the funds which were made available to the developing world were mostly in loans with an ongoing interest burden.

The developing world has experienced another major disadvantage over the years: it has had too little domestic savings. Indeed, in a recent report on development finance, the World Bank concluded that in the past 15 years or so, many developing countries have relied too much on external borrowing and too little on domestic resources. In Latin America, for example, domestic savings financed barely two thirds of gross domestic investment; in Africa, less than one half. In low-income and middle-income countries, external long-term debt increased by over 20 per cent annually in the 1970s and close to 15 per cent annually in the 1980s. In a sample of 38 developing countries for which relevant data existed, external debt at the end of 1986 exceeded domestic debt by more than 50 per cent. In the case of Latin America, external debt was, on average, two and a half times greater than domestic bank liabilities.

Despite the globalization of the world's financial system, it seems clear that the developing world as a whole cannot rely on external capital inflows only, and the outlook for attracting such funds is not encouraging. International commercial bank lending has virtually dried up and, in any case, is not an ideal form of financing long-term development. It probably will not be easily replaced by borrowing in international security markets: unpalatable as it may seem to the poorer countries, the financial liabilities of developing countries make them unattractive to private financial investors or private financial institutions. The outlook for official capital flows is also not good, as political opposition in the major donor countries appears to be hardening. Developing countries must therefore look more to foreign direct investment for an increasing proportion of their external financing.

While foreign direct investment is not cheap and has to be serviced by profit remittances, it carries with it considerable advantages, such as access to new technology and to new markets, and it bolsters competition in domestic markets. However, direct investment flourishes best in an environment of political and economic stability and is encouraged by liberal policies towards trade and capital. A change in attitude may therefore be required in many developing counties if they are to attract significant direct investment flows.

Domestic savings

This leads me to my final point, which cannot be stressed too strongly, namely, the need for developing countries to stimulate and mobilize domestic saving and to channel it into profitable uses. There is an urgent need in many developing countries to restructure domestic financial systems with this in mind.

Unfortunately, the need for an efficient financial intermediation system is not always fully recognized in many developing countries. In many of them, control over finance is regarded as an important tool of development strategy, so that governments typically intervene in the allocation of finance. Credit is often directed to priority projects with supposedly high economic and social returns—for example, into government-favoured industrial and agricultural projects or in directions that are expected to improve income distribution. Very often, interest rates on loans to favoured borrowers or projects are subsidized and fixed at well below market rates. Scarce foreign exchange is allocated to priority projects and provided at exchange rates bearing no relation to market equilibrium. Development financial institutions under State control may be set up to administer these policies, and more often than not, State operating enterprises are the most favoured client.

Experience has revealed many problems associated with directed credit and subsidized interest rate programmes. Subsidized interest rates place higher interest costs on other borrowers and also encourage low returns on the capital invested in favoured projects. Credit does not always reach the intended beneficiary but is sidetracked to larger, more influential borrowers, irrespective of return. Directed credit programmes also lead to the erosion of financial discipline and to the accumulation of non-performing loans which impede the long-term development of financial institutions. Moreover, when commercial banks are entitled to refinance with the central bank loans made to preferred sectors at below-market interest rates, excess money creation becomes endemic, leading to inflation. In turn, inflation is often associated with negative real interest rates which lead to low quality investment and discourage saving. Also, the high leveraging of firms, which is encouraged by artificially low interest rates, eventually leads to vulnerability in economic downturns and therefore to financial distress.

In its *World Development Report 1989,* the World Bank concluded that such practices have not favoured economic development, and it recommended that finance should cease to be a tool for implementing interventionist development strategies. Instead, developing countries should move to a voluntary market-based—that is, competitive—financial system. This would have the primary objectives of mobilizing domestic saving, which, as I have indicated earlier, will become an urgent necessity as external capital inflows become more restricted; increasing the availability of equity capital and long-term finance; making credit available to all classes of borrowers, subject, of course, to price; and ensuring that risks are reflected in returns.

You may think that I have diverged from the main topic of my paper—the globalization of financial markets and its implications for developing countries. However, it is my view that the globalization of financial markets is of much less significance to developing countries than the creation of more efficient domestic financial intermediation systems, and it seems clear to me that developing countries cannot take advantage of and participate in a globalized, international financial system as long as their own domestic financial systems remain in an embryonic and/or inefficient stage of development. I would like to quote the World Bank:

"A financial system provides services that are essential in a modern economy. The use of a stable, widely accepted medium of exchange reduces the cost of transactions. It facilitates trade, and therefore specialization in production. Financial assets with attractive yield, liquidity, and risk characteristics encourage saving in a financial form. By evaluating alternative investments and monitoring the activities of borrowers, financial intermediaries increase the efficiency of resource use. Access to a variety of financial instruments enables economic agents to pool, to price and to exchange risk. Trade, the efficient use of resources, saving, and risk are the cornerstones of a growing economy."

Of course, future growth depends on the economic policies and performance of the industrial countries, and clearly there is some need to reduce the huge economic imbalances among industrial countries; in particular, there is an urgent need for the United States to reduce its demands on the pool of world savings if more is to become available to the poorer countries. However, it is also clear that, in the last resort, the future growth of the developing countries depends largely on their own policies and efforts. Indeed, I think it is now well recognized by economists that the main difference between rich and poor countries lies less in the actual possession of natural resources than in the efficiency with which those resources are used; and a vital aspect of this is the mobilization of savings and the channelling of savings into growth-promoting investment. To this end, an effective financial intermediation system is of crucial importance.

Conclusions

Summarizing my main points, there is certainly a revolution going on towards the globalization of the financial markets of the industrialized countries. Perhaps the concept of one financial market is emerging with three corners: the United States, Japan and Europe. On the other hand, the developing world does not seem to be benefiting from this gigantic development.

If we want to stop the gap between the industrialized nations and the developing world from further widening, it is imperative that there be an increased capital flow from the industrialized countries to the developing countries in the form of direct investment, private bank lending and official development assistance to facilitate the growth of their economies.

The total funds needed by the world at large to achieve future growth greatly exceed the available sums for investments around the globe. In this connection, the huge deficits run by the United States greatly reduce the amount available for the rest of the world. Thus, the developing countries should greatly enhance their ability to attract foreign investments by generating confidence and promising attractive returns.

This emphasizes the ever-increasing requirement for substantially improving, revitalizing, upgrading, motivating and providing incentives for the productive use of human resources and management skills in the developing countries. It is manpower that can make the difference, not natural resources.

Finally, there is an urgent need to mobilize domestic savings in the developing countries and to channel them to well-managed and productive investments.

Chapter 4

THE CHALLENGE TO DEVELOPING COUNTRIES OF THE GLOBALIZATION OF FINANCIAL MARKETS

Nyum Jin[*]

Enormous changes are taking place in the global financial environment. Various factors changing the world's financial market are presenting challenges to financial market participants and regulatory authorities. Widespread programmes of financial liberalization have eliminated many of the institutional barriers to global finance, and technology has lowered the physical barriers imposed by nature. Advances in computing, information processing and telecommunications have expanded the volume of business. The reduction in transaction costs gives a wide range of market participants easy access to the same information simultaneously, facilitating the development of innovative financing techniques and expanding the scope of trading. International capital flows brought about by deregulation of exchange controls, variable exchange rates and fluctuating interest rates provide market participants with incentives to develop new financial instruments and techniques. All these factors have brought about competitive and structural changes in the financial environment.

*Vice-Minister of Finance, Republic of Korea.

Deregulation, technology and other common trends have induced a growing convergence of national financial systems in most advanced countries. Universal banks and specialized financial institutions, as well as institutional investors and securities markets, now play important roles in the financial systems of advanced countries.

Changing international financial markets

During the 1970s, the high and variable rates of inflation in advanced countries, coupled with technological developments, undermined many of the credit and banking controls then in use. In the early 1970s, several advanced countries, such as the United Kingdom, Canada and the Netherlands, enacted a series of wide-ranging financial reforms. Financial deregulation, which resumed in the late 1970s, ranged from the elimination or relaxation of controls on credit and foreign exchange to the removal of restrictions on the business activities of financial institutions. Interest rates on lending and wholesale deposits were liberalized. In most advanced countries, the changes were cautious and gradual. This contrasted sharply with the experience of the Southern Cone countries.

However, the stock market crisis of October 1987 caused many to reassess the old priorities in the development of the world financial system. Faced with these changes and risks, the countries of the European Community (EC) are making strenuous efforts to create a unified financial services market by the end of 1992. The Community's second banking coordination directive, which was adopted in December 1989, entitles banks licensed in any member country to provide a wide range of financial services throughout the Community under the home country's control without obtaining authorization from the host country. Banks will be permitted to engage in leasing, securities underwriting and trading and to offer portfolio management services. Furthermore, all of these services can be offered from across a member State's borders. Similar plans are being advanced for other types of financial institutions.

The EC member States are taking steps to prepare their financial institutions for the more competitive post-1992 environment, while some Governments are accelerating the deregulation of their own financial markets. In the EC's private sector, banks and other financial institutions are actively developing strategic plans based on the creation of the unified European market.

Increased competition, the opening of financial markets to insurers and money managers, and innovation in banking technology will probably lead to a shake-out. The upheaval in banking and finance may be greater than that confronting any other industry upon unification. Take-overs in the EC banking sector are also being carried out, along with growing participation by non-EC financial institutions.

In 1989, the United States and Canada began implementing a bilateral free trade agreement, which, among other things, would promote the expansion of financial institutions in those two countries.

Complementing the trend towards geographic integration, notably in the European Community and the United States, a general movement towards functional integration between financial markets is also under way among advanced countries. One of the major developments has been the gradual spread of universal banking-type structures to various industrialized countries. In many cases, governmental authorities in the advanced countries have relaxed functional constraints in order to promote competition and greater market efficiency. In the United Kingdom and Canada, for example, recent measures have allowed commercial banks to purchase or establish securities companies and related businesses.

Financial reforms in Latin American countries

Financial innovation and deregulation in the United Kingdom, the United States and other developed countries appear to have encouraged financial liberalization in developing countries.

Beginning in the mid-1970s, the Southern Cone countries of Latin America (Argentina, Chile and Uruguay) implemented extensive and radical economic liberalization. The important element was financial deregulation in which State-owned financial institutions were denationalized, interest rates were liberalized to be determined in financial markets, controls on asset management by banks were lifted and foreign banks were permitted to operate in domestic financial markets. However, contrary to the initial expectation, the financial liberalization efforts of the Southern Cone countries ended in the renationalization of banks, reimposition of regulations and chaotic financial markets. For one thing, the three Southern Cone countries that undertook economic liberalization were afflicted by serious inflation, unemployment and balance-of-payment problems.

The available studies on the Southern Cone experiences with economic liberalization in the 1970s reveal that financial deregulation complicated macroeconomic management, as it created incentives for destabilizing behaviour on the part of banks. Financial deregulation did not help to establish a competitive market structure in the financial sector, but resulted, instead, in the domination of financial institutions by large non-financial economic groups, and this was responsible for the lack of discipline in the banking industry. Financial deregulation had an undesirable effect in that it dried up long-term finance in the three countries.

While these undesirable consequences of financial deregulation were serious, many analysts of the Southern Cone experience point out that the undisciplined behaviour of financial intermediaries was critical in bringing down the whole liberalization programme. Another explanation for the failure of the programme finds fault with the pace of financial deregulation, which, in all three countries, may have been too rapid and abrupt for banks to adjust to the new financial market environment.

In both Chile and Argentina, reduced credibility had considerable effects on the outcome of the reforms. The inability to establish consistency between fiscal and financial policies has, many times, caused reform credibility crises in the Southern Cone countries. One lesson to be drawn from the experience of those countries is that policy makers should always pay special attention to the establishment of credibility when implementing financial liberalization reforms.

Financial liberalization in Korea

Korea waited until internal and external macroeconomic imbalances were largely eliminated before undertaking major liberalization reforms. However, Korea was still faced with the problem of determining the sequence and speed of individual market liberalization required for an optimal transition to a fully liberalized economy.

In Korea, domestic financial deregulation and trade liberalization have been pursued more or less simultaneously, as part of a rather long, ongoing process. In each sector, a step-by-step approach has been adopted, phasing in specific liberalization measures according to the associated urgency, convenience or constraints, as perceived by policy makers.

Financial liberalization efforts started with the lifting of many restrictions on bank management in order to promote competition and efficiency. Detailed regulations governing the organizational, budgetary, branching and business practices of banks which did not promote prudential supervision were relaxed. More significantly, between 1981 and 1983, the Government divested its equity shares in all nationwide city banks, transferring ownership to private hands.

In order to promote competition in the financial markets, entry barriers were lowered. Financial services provided by different intermediaries were diversified and made increasingly to overlap.

Progress has also been made in the area of monetary and credit management. By June 1982, most preferential interest rates applying to various policy loans had been abolished, making it easier to scale down policy loans. The relative share of policy loans has declined since the authorities reduced the National Investment Fund and, more recently, automatic short-term export credit. Another significant step taken in early 1984 was allowing financial intermediaries, within a given range, to determine their own lending rates according to the creditworthiness of borrowers.

Fortunately, the changing economic environment has provided favourable conditions for interest rate deregulation in Korea. First, low and stable inflation since 1983 and high national savings in excess of domestic investment have narrowed the disparity between regulated and free market rates. Secondly, with successful industrialization leading to the recent current account surpluses, Korean industries are generally believed to be competitive enough to remain strong without the effective subsidies of interest rate controls. In the presence of interest rate controls, Korea's freer external capital flows would undermine domestic monetary stability more seriously.

Against this background, most bank and non-bank lending rates and some long-term deposit rates were decontrolled early in December 1989. Deregulated interest rates or yields also included those on financial debentures, corporate bonds, asset management accounts and funds, and such money market instruments as certificates of deposit (CDs) and certificates of payment (CPs). Rates on some policy loans were not deregulated, and short-term deposit rates are now still controlled for fear of excessive competition among financial intermediaries. To prevent any massive transfer of funds to liberalized financial assets, restrictions were imposed in the form of a minimum transaction unit (CP) and ceilings on the handling of some businesses (CDs and asset management accounts and funds).

The results of interest rate deregulation have so far fallen short of expectations. Bank lending rates and most rates in the primary securities market are still very rigid and unresponsive to market conditions, indicating that the Korean financial market is still far from being fully integrated and operating on a purely competitive basis. This phenomenon seems to be partly due to limited interest rate deregulation and partly to inertia and the persistence of a backward-looking mentality, from a time when most financial institutions were run like public enterprises.

External liberalization

An initial step towards opening the capital market was taken in 1981 with the establishment of international trust funds. Two corporate-type funds—the Korea Fund and the Korea-Europe Fund—were launched in 1984 and 1987, respectively. Since 1985, Korean companies have issued convertible bonds in overseas markets. In December 1988, a timetable was announced for opening the capital market to foreigners and for allowing domestic investors to purchase foreign securities. According to the timetable, beginning in 1992 foreign investors will be allowed to buy stocks in the domestic market. In 1991, foreign securities firms will be able to open branch offices or joint ventures.

The maximum permissible equity participation of foreign securities firms in an existing Korean securities company was increased from 5 per cent to 10 per cent individually and from 10 per cent to 40 per cent collectively. Foreign investors will be permitted to sell stocks converted from corporate bonds (CBs) among themselves in the over-the-counter market, and these CB-converted stocks may be traded on the Korean Stock Exchange beginning in 1991.

In conjunction with the opening of the domestic capital market, the Government plans to gradually liberalize overseas securities investment by Korean investors. Overseas securities investment funds will be expanded, and restrictions on overseas investment by institutional investors will continue to be relaxed.

Before fully opening the capital market, it is essential that domestic interest and exchange rates be deregulated and stabilized on the basis of an efficient market system. For the exchange rate to reflect the demand and supply situation of the market, foreign exchange controls should be relaxed in a way that will broaden the base of the market. In line with the relaxation of foreign exchange controls and the broadening of the foreign exchange market, the exchange rate will increasingly have to reflect market forces. Furthermore, in order to minimize any disturbances that might be caused by opening the capital market, Korea should enhance the operative efficiency of the market beforehand. Strengthening institutional investors is essential in this regard. Systems for corporate disclosure, external auditing and credit ratings have yet to be firmly established in Korea. In the still shallow market, regulations on insider trading, price manipulations and other unfair transactions are not yet effective.

The Korean market will be increasingly open to foreign investors and financial institutions, while Korean financial intermediaries will also increasingly find their way to international financial markets to meet the needs of their customers under the new environment of relaxed regulations on foreign exchange and capital transactions. This progress in external financial liberalization will have important implications for reshaping the Korean financial system.

Towards more open financial markets

A number of countries, both advanced and developing, have taken measures during the past decade to liberalize their financial systems. The pace and scope of financial reform have differed considerably from country to country. Financial reforms have been undertaken in international as well as domestic financial markets. Many advanced countries have reduced their capital controls and eased restrictions on the entry of foreign financial institutions. The greater international mobility of capital, the globalization of financial markets and the development of new financial instruments have rendered a closed financial policy costly and quite ineffective. In varying degrees, developing countries have participated in the trend towards more open and integrated financial markets, partly in response to the growing economic integration through trade.

Internationalization of financial markets has certain advantages for developing countries. Foreign competition forces domestic financial intermediaries to be more efficient and to broaden the range of services they offer. It can also facilitate the transfer of financial technology to developing countries. But opening financial markets also causes problems. If it is done prematurely or too rapidly, it can cause volatile financial flows that can aggravate domestic instability. Internationalization means giving up a large degree of autonomy in domestic monetary and financial policy.

Conclusions

In view of potential problems with financial liberalization, there are certain institutional reforms that developing countries should implement before moving to deep financial liberalization. The first reform would be to introduce safeguards to keep the relationships between large business groups and the banks at arm's length in order to prevent the large business groups from dominating the banking system. The second reform would be the development of non-bank financial intermediaries which could be subject to less government control. Liberalization should not be limited to the reform of the banking system, but should also aim to develop a more broadly based financial system which includes capital markets and non-bank financial institutions. Liberalization may begin with these financial institutions, so that they could compete in, and eventually integrate with, the organized financial system and informal credit markets. They will increase pressure for further liberalization and promote the deregulation of the banking system. A well-balanced and competitive financial system contributes to macroeconomic stability by strengthening the system in the face of external and internal shocks.

With financial intermediaries expanding the range of services they offer and operating in an environment of more competition and less government protection, the financial market is likely to experience excessive instability. Institutional safeguards should therefore be introduced to reduce this instability and maintain an efficient financial system. Prudential regulation should be strengthened, and an institutional framework for efficient restructuring of troubled financial intermediaries should be developed.

By providing various rules of sound banking practices, such as maintaining capital adequacy and limiting credit concentration, prudential regulation helps banks avoid insolvency. Prudential regulation is also essential for the development of a healthy capital market. Its major tasks are to enhance transparency in the market and to adequately control price manipulation and other unfair transactions. To keep up with the expansion of business boundaries for financial intermediaries, as well as with the innovation and sophistication of financial technology, the supervisory system has to be strengthened, and the divided supervisory functions should be integrated under a more comprehensive supervisory body.

In order to survive and prosper in changing international financial markets, financial intermediaries themselves will have to restructure and implement significant changes in their strategies. Such restructuring will have to be supported by modifications in regulatory systems and practices.

Chapter 5

FINANCIAL GLOBALIZATION AND INSTABILITY

Yilmaz Akyüz*

The past two decades have seen increased financial integration of national economies and globalization of finance. At the same time, the international monetary and financial system has exhibited disorderly and sometimes even chaotic behaviour, as witnessed by many sharp and unpredictable shifts in the major monetary and financial variables, including the prices of financial assets, interest and exchange rates, and flows of capital, both across borders and across markets for financial assets denominated in different currencies. There have also been periods in which these variables have persistently stayed at levels not compatible with their fundamental determinants; instability has thus been latent even when it has not actually occurred. As a result, serious strains have been put on international debtor-creditor relations, the banking system, capital markets and international trade, payments and exchange arrangements.

Until the early 1980s, this behaviour could plausibly be explained by shocks and abrupt changes in the environment in which the international monetary and financial system operated. First, the early 1970s saw progressive disintegration and the eventual breakdown of the Bretton

*Senior Analyst, United Nations Conference on Trade and Development. This paper was written before the start of the Gulf crisis in August 1990 and the subsequent turmoil in financial markets. The author is grateful to Detlef Kotte for his contribution to section C and to Andreas Marinakis for his assistance in section A.

Woods system; currency market turbulence and exchange rate instability could thus be expected to persist until floating was generalized and the markets learned and established new rules of the game. Secondly, the inflationary experience following the oil-price rises of the 1970s had destabilizing influences for the international monetary and financial system. On the one hand, not only did foreign exchange markets have to operate under conditions of price instability, but also relative price levels of major countries underwent drastic changes. On the other hand, the trade imbalances that emerged as a result of oil-price increases and terms-of-trade changes, together with policies designed to avoid contraction in economic activity, resulted in substantial increases in international liquidity and debt-financing of current account deficits which proved a major problem subsequently. Finally, the disinflationary process of the late 1970s and early 1980s entailed substantial instability in financial and currency markets because the mix and stance of policies in the major countries gave rise to large swings in key financial prices. The pace of disinflation also differed among the major countries, implying substantial changes in relative price levels.

However, such conjunctural and transitory factors are much less capable of explaining the continued instability in international money and finance over the last six to eight years. This period has seen neither especially high inflation nor serious supply shocks, and the major market economies have increasingly converged in their growth performance and displayed increased willingness to undertake joint interventions to manage exchange rates. Even so, the international monetary and financial system has remained unstable. As pointed out by the President of the Federal Reserve Bank of New York, in the Winter 1989–90 issue of the Bank's *Quarterly Review*: "The past fifteen years have witnessed a greater number of financial disruptions with potential systemic implications than was the case over the post-war period prior to 1974. And if we divide the 1974–1989 period roughly in half, the latter half of that interval has seen more disruption than the former."

These considerations suggest that deficiencies in the structure of the international financial and monetary system and in the philosophy underlying policies are more important factors in the observed behaviour of financial and currency markets. While market behaviour and the conduct of policies in the major countries have tended to generate destabilizing influences, the increased internationalization of finance has enhanced the scope for propagation of disturbances from one market to another within as well as across borders. Thus, three basic deficiencies appear to underlie the increased instability.

The first deficiency stems from the fact that the main activity of financial markets has become not so much to intermediate between ultimate savers and investors, to allocate resources on the basis of asset valuations reflecting long-term risk and profits, and to facilitate transactions and payments needed for investment, trade and production, but rather to create short-term opportunities for speculation in volatile and misaligned asset valuations.

The second deficiency is that the policy approach prevailing in the major countries has also tended to contribute to instability in many ways. Since the beginning of the decade many countries have effectively ceased to use the government budget and price and income policies for macroeconomic management, thereby overloading monetary policy and making different policy objectives more difficult to reconcile. In addition, the conduct of monetary policy has changed significantly; not only have interest rates been deregulated, but, except at times of serious disruptions, monetary policy has been directed at certain monetary aggregates rather than the management of financial asset prices and interest rates. Consequently, monetary and real shocks have tended to generate sharp swings in financial asset prices and interest rates. Furthermore, interest rate deregulation has not always been accompanied by increased prudential regulations; excessive risk-taking in the financial system has played a major role in financial failures in some major countries. Finally, the dismantling of quantitative and tax restrictions on movements of capital across countries, markets and currencies has accorded markets greater scope to generate and/or propagate speculative disturbances.

The third deficiency is that effective multilateral constraints and obligations on policy-making in the major countries have been absent. Although existing institutional arrangements have been outmoded by the increased financial integration and internationalization of finance that has taken place, there has been no reform designed to ensure effective multilateral surveillance over the policies of countries which have a large impact on the world economy.

Disruptions and disorder in financial markets have so far been contained in that they have not led to crises with serious and widespread damage for the real economy. However, crisis management has been costly. For instance, an international banking crisis has been staved off at the expense of living standards, stability and development in debtor developing countries, while exchange rate management has tended to raise world interest rates. More important, so long as the international monetary and financial system remains structurally vulnerable, the potential for an extremely costly crisis will remain. Again, in the words of the President of the Federal Reserve Bank of New York: "If a crisis were to develop . . . its capacity to generate major damage to the real economy may be greater today than it was in the past. The fundamental reason for this is the nature, speed and complexity of the operational, liquidity and credit interdependences that bind together all major financial institutions and markets in the world."

This paper analyses the deficiencies in the international financial and monetary system and points to possible ways of dealing with them.

A

INTERNATIONAL FINANCIAL INTEGRATION

The nature and volume of international finance

Strictly speaking, the term "domestic finance" covers only financial transactions among residents denominated in the country's own currency (the "home currency"). By contrast, international finance involves either a non-resident or assets denominated in a foreign currency, or both, that is, financial transactions across borders or across currencies. International banking thus involves claims and liabilities *vis-à-vis* residents denominated in foreign currencies, as well as claims and liabilities *vis-à-vis* non-residents denominated in either home or foreign currencies.

This definition of international finance is wider than Eurocurrency or offshore banking, which excludes international bank loans to and deposits of non-residents denominated in the home currency. It also includes bond and equity issues in Eurobond and Euroequity markets—that is, in a currency not that of the country in which the bond or the equity is issued; issues in the so-called foreign bond markets—that is, bonds issued by non-residents in a country in the currency of that country; and non-resident holdings of securities issued by residents in the home currency—that is, issued in the so-called national stock market.

However, domestic and international transactions are not segmented into separate markets. When the financial market of a country is opened to non-resident investors and/or borrowers, or when residents are allowed to deal in foreign currency assets and liabilities, these markets become internationalized. As national and international financial transactions develop relations of substitutability and complementarity, financial transactions with purely domestic characteristics become subject to strong external influences.

The share of transactions with international characteristics can, in principle, provide a good indicator of the exposure to such influences. In 11 industrial countries—Belgium, Canada, France, Germany, Italy, Ireland, Japan, the Netherlands, Switzerland, the United Kingdom and the United States—and eight offshore centres—the Bahamas, Bahrain, the Cayman Islands, Hong Kong, Lebanon, the Netherlands Antilles, Panama and Singapore—taken together, almost one third of total bank assets qualifies as international. The share is very large in some countries—two thirds in the United Kingdom and more than three quarters in offshore centres—but relatively low in Germany. About two thirds of international assets are interbank transactions. In general, claims on non-residents in foreign currencies account for a substantial portion of international assets, but banks in the United States and Germany appear to have a stronger preference for the home currency in international lending.

The combined size of world financial markets can be estimated at over $36,000 billion, half of which is accounted for by commercial banks. Assets which are strictly international—that is, international bank assets, Euroequities, Eurobonds and foreign bonds—account for 18 per cent of total world markets; but including those "national" capital markets which have become more open to non-resident investors substantially raises the share of world financial markets having an international character.

In the 1980s there was a major shift in international financial intermediation from banking to security markets ("securitization"). International bank lending slowed down, reflecting the cut-back of lending to developing countries and the increased recourse of international borrowers to direct security issues while Eurobond markets became important; Euroequity markets also emerged. While securitization has reduced the share of international banking in world financial markets, it has increased the involvement of banks in security transactions, greatly widening the grey area between banking and security market transactions, often in the form of off-balance-sheet business. Securitization has gone hand in hand with the introduction of a variety of new financial instruments designed to reduce investors' exposure to credit, liquidity and exchange rate risk.

The internationalization of finance has also meant financial deepening at the global level. Growth in world output, trade and investment naturally tends to cause the volume of financial transactions to grow. However, over the last two or three decades the pace of growth of international financial transactions has been far in excess of that of the real variables.

Since the early 1970s, international banking has grown at more than 20 per cent per annum, or about twice as fast as international trade (12 per cent) and world output (10 per cent). Between 1972 and

1987, world trade increased by about $2,500 billion, while international banking expanded by $4,000 billion.

A comparison of finance with capital accumulation would provide an even better measure of financial deepening in view of the role of finance in converting savings into investment. Between 1982 and 1988, the average annual increment in the stock of world financial assets was about $3,800 billion, while the annual average level of world fixed capital formation was around $2,300 billion. The ratio of the size of the international banking market to total global fixed investment doubled in less than a decade.

Deregulation and internationalization of finance

The strong tendency for the pace of the internationalization of finance to outstrip the growth of real activity has been facilitated by developments in communication and transportation technology, particularly electronics. These have allowed information to be acquired, processed and disseminated much more rapidly and at very low cost and to greatly improve payments-transmission mechanisms across countries. As a result, opportunities for cross-border arbitrage have increased, the costs of international financial transactions have been reduced and national markets have been brought closer together.

The progressive dismantling of policy barriers to capital movements has also played a cardinal role. Financial deregulation and liberalization quickened after the collapse of the Bretton Woods system and further accelerated in the 1980s. As a result, the financial system prevailing in the major countries now has the following broad characteristics: cross-border and foreign exchange credits are virtually unrestricted in all the countries concerned; cross-border and foreign exchange deposits are allowed in all major financial centres and are being liberalized in others, for example, in some member countries of the European Community; and security transactions now enjoy a high degree of freedom.

Since the early 1970s, freedom of capital movements has been increasingly viewed as an important policy objective. This trend is in stark contrast to government attitudes in the post-war years: the Bretton Woods era was based on a consensus that capital flows unrelated to foreign direct investment or trade should be discouraged or even prevented. By contrast, in the field of trade, restrictions of various kinds have proliferated. The tendency for financial policies to become less restrictive cannot be explained by considerations of efficiency; if any, the efficiency argument has greater validity in respect of trade liberalization. A more plausible reason is that costs of financial openness, such as loss of policy autonomy and increased financial instability, being collective, are anonymous in their incidence, whereas the benefits accrue to particular economic agents, especially international financial and non-financial enterprises and rentiers. Political pressures by the latter for financial opening therefore do not meet significant resistance. By contrast, in the field of trade, it is the costs of restrictiveness that are borne collectively, and the benefits accrue to particular groups.

The failure of controls imposed under the Bretton Woods system to check capital movements and to slow down the growth of unregulated offshore markets and relocation of financial activities also played an important role in changing official attitudes towards financial deregulation. This entailed a more liberal treatment of financial operations in order to avoid a loss of competitiveness for domestic financial institutions. Similarly, competition among national financial markets has been an important factor in the proliferation of deregulation and a more liberal treatment of finance. Examples include competitive abolition of withholding tax on financial assets held by non-residents; widespread decisions concerning non-resident issues in national capital markets; authorization given to foreign banks to lead-manage bond issues; and removal of restrictions on trading in certain financial instruments. When many major financial centres deregulate, the rest have little choice but to follow suit. The process tends to be circular and cumulative also because markets themselves generate pressures for further freedom, for deregulation generates fluctuations and turnover for many financial operators on which their profits depend.

Moreover, there has been a tendency for national financial regulations to become subject to international negotiations and agreements. These include the move towards a unified single market within the European Community; the Canada-United States Free Trade Agreement of 1989, which provides for the removal of restrictions on United States financial institutions operating in Canada and equal treatment of Canadian banks in the United States; and the 1984 United States-Japan agreement, which contributed to a massive increase in the Japanese portfolio and foreign direct investment in the United States instead of increasing the penetration of Japanese financial markets by United States institutions. So far, such agreements have been at the regional or bilateral level, but financial services are on the agenda of the current multilateral trade negotiations.

Financial openness in developing countries

In developing countries, the degree of financial openness—that is, the ease with which residents can acquire assets and liabilities in foreign exchange and non-residents can operate in national financial markets—is not accurately reflected by the restrictiveness of regulations ostensibly in force. The administrative capacity to implement rules and regulations effectively is often lacking, and the underdevelopment of financial intermediaries and the importance of informal financial ("curb") markets make it relatively easy to circumvent regulations.

The degree of financial openness also depends on specific national factors. For instance, a high level of earnings from tourism and workers' remittances facilitates the formation of a curb market in foreign currency. Similarly, the presence of transnational corporations, whether in financial or non-financial sectors, makes it easier to transfer funds in and out, as does physical proximity to hard-currency countries and financial havens. For example, in Uruguay, where banks are free to accept foreign exchange deposits and banking secrecy prevails, about one half of foreign exchange deposits—which account for about 80 per cent of total bank deposits—belong to Argentinians.

Other examples can also be cited of how liberal treatment of financial inflows abroad can impede a country from limiting its degree of financial openness. The United States, for instance, exempts foreign depositors from taxation. Until the recent tax reform in Mexico, this, in combination with the tax deductibility of interest payments in that country, gave enterprises an incentive to shift their funds abroad and recycle them back as loans to themselves or to enterprises under their control, thereby avoiding taxes on interest income received in the United States while deducting interest payments on loans from their taxable income in Mexico.

Nevertheless, a country's own policies and regulations also play a major role in determining the degree of financial openness. Since the early 1970s there has been, in general, an easing of restrictions on the access of residents to loans from international markets; on portfolio investment of residents in foreign currency assets at home and abroad; and on the access of non-residents to domestic capital markets. Although some countries have subsequently reimposed restrictions because of the adverse consequences for external indebtedness and capital flight, developing countries generally have become much more open financially.

The first wave of liberalization in developing countries generally took the form of allowing the private sector to borrow abroad. This happened not only in the Southern Cone countries in Latin America— Argentina, Chile and Uruguay—after the mid-1970s in the context of broader programmes of financial deregulation, but also in a number of countries where domestic financial markets continued to be highly regulated—for example, Turkey, Yugoslavia and the Philippines. Domestic banks were often involved as intermediaries between international capital markets and domestic borrowers, often raising funds in the former to extend to the latter in the domestic currency. In many cases, particularly in the Southern Cone countries, the need for government approval and guarantee was lifted on the grounds that private firms would assess the costs and benefits of domestic and foreign debt equally carefully, since their survival depended on it.

The freedom to borrow triggered a massive build-up of foreign exchange liabilities in the private financial and non-financial sectors, particularly in countries where borrowers continued to enjoy exchange rate guarantees or where domestic interest rates rose sharply, which they often did as a result of deregulation. The consequent overborrowing by the private sector contributed significantly to the subsequent debt-servicing difficulties and the debt crisis. In many such countries, governments found it necessary to subsidize private debt-servicing through special exchange rates or to assume the liabilities of insolvent financial institutions. Controls over foreign borrowing by the private sector were subsequently reinstated in many such countries. Resident banks are now generally allowed to hold short-term foreign exchange liabilities *vis-à-vis* international capital markets provided they are for financing trade and covered by short-term foreign exchange claims on exporters.

The liberalization episode in the 1970s, particularly in Latin America, also included relaxation of restrictions on convertibility and capital movements. In some cases, this went even further than in some major industrialized countries. This, in combination with inappropriate exchange and interest rate policies, gave rise to a substantial outflow of capital. Restrictions had to be reimposed, but capital flight continued, particularly in the early years of the debt crisis. The cumulative outflow of capital from Latin America during the period 1977–1983 has been estimated at over $100 billion. There can be little doubt that an important part of it was channelled to financial markets and institutions in the major industrial countries, particularly the United States, and constituted part of the category of "assets with international characteristics" described above; in 1988, the total liabilities of the banks in the United States to non-bank foreigners amounted to $87 billion, with the residents of countries such as Argentina and, particularly, Mexico holding larger amounts of deposits in United States banks than, say, Brazil, where capital controls were much tighter.

While a large majority of developing countries have restrictions on capital outflows, there has been an increased tendency to permit and encourage holding of foreign exchange deposits with resident banks.

Previously, many developing countries in which remittances from workers abroad were sizeable had already offered such deposits to non-resident nationals at attractive terms in order to divert foreign exchange from curb markets. However, during the 1980s many countries also allowed residents to hold foreign exchange deposits in resident banks and offered interest rates above world levels. These deposits are very liquid and are accessible even to the moderately wealthy. They often enjoy full government guarantees and, in some countries, deposit holders are also allowed to transfer limited sums abroad to cover certain types of spending, for example, tourism. On the other hand, many countries have also permitted exporters to retain part of their export receipts in the form of foreign currency deposits and to use them to finance imports without being subject to foreign exchange restrictions.

Whereas in most major developed countries bank liabilities to non-bank residents denominated in foreign currency have barely exceeded 10 per cent of total bank liabilities, in several developing countries the share of foreign exchange deposits in total deposits has grown rapidly to reach very high levels, even exceeding the share of deposits in the home currency—for example, about 20 per cent of the total in Chile and between 40 and 60 per cent in Bolivia, Costa Rica, the Philippines, Turkey and Yugoslavia. This substantial increase in banks' liabilities having international characteristics represents an ongoing process of currency substitution that undermines autonomy in monetary policy and has been brought about by increased resort to currency depreciations, heightened macroeconomic instability and increased risks and uncertainty regarding returns on domestic currency assets.

In recent years there has also been increased access of non-residents to financial markets in developing countries. Deregulation of domestic financial markets has often been accompanied by relaxing restrictions on the entry of foreign banks. Of equal or even greater importance is the substantially increased access of non-residents to national equity markets. Some countries have encouraged this, often within the context of privatization programmes, in order both to acquire foreign currency and to generate private demand for public assets; such demand is often small relative to the size of the enterprises to be sold off. In some cases, the development of the domestic capital markets has also been a goal.

Resort to various debt-conversion facilities by developing countries has significantly raised the amount of equities and domestic currency debt-assets held by non-residents. In some countries residents have also been allowed to buy foreign currency in the curb market to repurchase debt in secondary markets, and such schemes have often included tax and other forms of amnesty in order to bring back flight capital. Similarly, re-lending and on-lending facilities have served to reallocate the external liabilities of the country among various sectors, often from the public to the private sector, establishing direct links between the latter and external creditors. The "market-based menu" has raised the degree of financial openness by opening up new prospects for international arbitrage and speculation for both residents and non-residents in debtor countries.

B
SOME CONSEQUENCES OF THE INTERNATIONALIZATION OF FINANCE

Capital mobility, speculation and rates of return

The main argument in favour of financial openness and internationalization of finance is that it would improve the allocation of resources internationally. If allowed to move freely, capital would flow to countries in response to opportunities for real investment, thereby equalizing rates of return on investment everywhere, and would allow individual countries either to save more than they invest or to invest more than they save, according to market disciplines.

Whether openness and internationalization in practice have had these results can, in principle, be assessed in three ways: by comparing rates of returns on physical capital; by comparing returns on similar financial assets; and by examining the links between national savings and investment rates.

Comparison of rates of return on capital investment among the Group of Seven countries shows that, on average, inter-country differences in rates of return (as measured by the coefficient of variation) were as large during the 1980s as they were during the 1960s and early 1970s.

Lowering of national barriers to financial flows has undoubtedly reduced substantially the degree of segmentation of financial markets and, hence, international dispersion of prices for financial assets denominated in the same currency but issued in different countries. Rapid dissemination of information, increased ease of market access and greatly reduced transaction costs have helped equalize yields on assets denominated in the same currency and with identical default risk and term to maturity in various parts of integrated financial markets—for example, dollar certificates of deposit issued by London and New York banks.

But a similar tendency is not discernible for financial assets with identical risk and maturity characteristics but different currency denominations—for example, United States Treasury bills in dollars and United Kingdom Treasury bills in sterling—even though certain financial intermediaries, institutional investors and large corporations accounting for an important part of the market find them close substitutes. The interest rate differential between two such assets should indicate that the currency in which the asset offering a higher rate of interest is denominated will depreciate against the other currency, over the same time interval as the maturity of the assets, so as to equalize the rates of return on the two assets, expressed in a common currency. But this has not been the case, especially in the 1980s; for example, during the first half of the 1980s, the dollar offered higher interest rates and sold at a discount in the forward markets against most other currencies, and yet dollar depreciation failed to materialize within the time-frame of the contracts entered into; again, some European currencies have persistently offered higher interest rates *and* appreciated against the others during the same interval of time—for example, the French franc against the Swiss franc during recent years. These strongly suggest that markets systematically leave opportunities for abnormal profits un-exploited and that they are inefficient in the sense that they fail to incorporate relevant information in the determination of exchange rates.

This, together with the fact that nominal exchange rates do not move in line with the purchasing power parity of the two currencies, means that real interest rates have not tended to be equalized across countries. Disparities in real interest rates among major countries are also reflected in differences in the cost of capital. Firms in the United States and the United Kingdom suffer from a decided disadvantage in this respect, compared to those in the Federal Republic of Germany and Japan, and need a higher rate of return on their investment in order to cover financing costs.

This last observation also suggests a relatively strong link between national savings and investment. Indeed, direct evidence on this link is in line with the evidence on relative rates of return and interest rates. They suggest that even among the member countries of the Organisa-tion for Economic Cooperation and Development (OECD), where capital has become increasingly mobile, the strength of the correlation between national savings and investment rates has not diminished and a very large share of new domestic savings tends to remain at home.

This does not necessarily mean that financial markets are not inte-grated or that capital is not very mobile: to gauge the degree of financial integration and capital mobility in terms of the extent to which rates of return are equalized reflects a priori assumptions about the role of international finance which may not necessarily tally with reality. Mas-sive flows of capital are not always motivated by opportunities for real investment. Indeed, a very large proportion of international financial transactions today is unrelated to trade and investment. The daily vol-ume of foreign exchange trading in major currency markets has reached almost the average monthly volume of world trade. International capi-tal flows reflect portfolio decisions rather than business decisions—for example, a decision to establish a production base in a foreign country.

The annual increase in the size of the international banking market alone now amounts to almost nine times total foreign direct investment made across all borders. Since a large proportion of transactions in the international banking market represents cross-border transactions, this evidence alone implies that capital flows across countries have little to do with investment. Besides, annual increases in cross-border banking transactions are several times greater than the annual net capital flows across countries.

These transactions have increasingly come to be governed by perceptions of prospects of short-term capital gains and losses rather than long-term yields, and are capable of generating gyrations in exchange rates and security prices. These, in turn, increase profit opportunities and, hence, the speculative component of the market. It is far from clear that the process of international financial deepening is contributing to efficiency in the allocation of resources internationally, and it appears that the degree of financial deepening has gone beyond the point needed for trade and investment. This is, indeed, what Keynes foresaw would happen as financial markets developed:

> "If I may be allowed to appropriate the term 'speculation' for the activity of forecasting the psychology of the market, and the term 'enterprise' for the activity of forecasting the prospective yield of assets over their whole life, it is by no means always the case that speculation predominates over enterprise. As the organization of investment markets improves, the risk of the predominance of speculation does, however, increase. . . Speculators may do no harm as bubbles on a steady stream of enterprise. But the position is serious when enterprise becomes the bubble on a whirlpool of speculation. When the capital development of a country becomes a by-product of the activities of a casino, the job is likely to be ill-done. The measure of success attained by Wall Street, regarded as an institution of which the proper social purpose is to direct new investment into the most profitable channels in terms of future yield, cannot be claimed as one of the outstanding triumphs of laissez-faire capitalism—which is not surprising, if I am right in thinking that the best brains of Wall Street have been in fact directed towards a different object."[1]

Links between currency and financial markets

The internationalization of finance and the integration of financial markets have considerably increased the importance of securing an exchange rate system conducive to financial stability. For one thing, the increased denomination of assets and liabilities of financial intermediaries, debtors and investors in foreign currencies means that the value of assets and liabilities is directly influenced by exchange rate changes. For another, events in exchange markets can exert a strong influence on bond and equity prices because changes in exchange rate expectations can induce funds to be shifted among securities denominated in different currencies, and/or because policy measures taken to manage exchange rates or to deal with the inflationary or deflationary influences of exchange rate changes alter interest rates and security prices. Exchange rate instability and uncertainty can therefore increase the level of risk in the financial system. For instance, banks can incur substantial losses when there is a serious mismatch between currency denomination of their assets and liabilities, and many governments in major countries have introduced regulations restricting open positions. However, perfect matching—for example, by taking forward cover—is very difficult and costly, particularly since bank liabilities are much shorter in maturity and their currency composition can undergo sharp changes. For these reasons, regulations do not generally require perfect matching since this would imply serious restrictions on the ability of banks to accept foreign exchange deposits and, hence, loss of international business.

The impact of unexpected changes, and hence uncertainty, cannot be fully removed unless there are forward markets for all goods and assets for which there are current markets, and they reach far into the future. Since there are not, the financial system is subject to a systemic risk. Existing forward and futures markets and instruments simply transfer risk to those who are willing to take it at a price, rather than eliminate risk by providing guidance as to the future course of prices; these instruments are used as much for gambling as for hedging. Risk transfer may be possible for each operator taken individually, but not collectively, because the quality of assets held by financial intermediaries or savers investing in direct securities will remain vulnerable to unexpected changes in exchange rates since their debtors cannot be fully covered. As noted by the General Manager of the Bank for International Settlements: "You may argue that when risk-averse market participants shift risks associated with unexpected interest and exchange rate developments onto willing risk takers, everybody is going to be better off. This may well be the case, but increased collective happiness does not necessarily mean greater systemic stability."[2]

The effects of monetary policy and interest rates on exchange rates are familiar: changes in interest rate differentials (current and/or expected) can lead to massive shifts of portfolios among financial assets denominated in different currencies, exerting a significant influence on exchange rates. What is less appreciated is the influence of changes in expected exchange rates on prices of securities denominated in different currencies and, hence, on interest rates. These effects occur because, as noted above, the demand for securities denominated in different currencies depends, *inter alia,* on expected exchange rates. Changes in expectations can thus shift portfolios between bonds and equities denominated in different currencies, even causing sharp changes in their prices, as well as in current exchange rates. Such shifts can generate disparate movements in the prices of securities in different countries, as occurred between New York and Tokyo in the early months of 1990.

It is important to stress that the shifts in question are in the *stock* of financial wealth, not merely in the *flow* of external savings as measured by current account deficits, which are very small in comparison and do not have a significant influence on domestic interest rates. Moreover, portfolio shifts from, say, yen-denominated to dollar-denominated securities can occur and alter the exchange rates and their relative prices significantly, quite independently of current account balances and the flow of external savings between the two countries concerned.

Similarly, policy responses to developments in currency markets can generate changes in security prices. Management of exchange rates under conditions of strong market pressures tends to generate considerable swings in bond prices and interest rates, particularly when domestic monetary policy is targeting certain reserve aggregates and exchange market intervention needs to be sterilized through domestic open-market operations. Alternatively, when sterilization is too difficult, action may be needed on discount and/or interbank rates to check liquidity expansion. When pressures on the currency markets are due to serious inconsistencies in the mix and stance of macroeconomic policies in major countries, attempts to manage exchange rates through monetary policy and currency market intervention can prove highly destabilizing for the financial system, as exemplified by the events leading to the October 1987 crash.

Exchange rate management and/or trade adjustment can introduce a bias towards higher interest rates. If the burden of responsibility for policy action is put entirely on deficit countries and monetary policy is the only tool, defending the exchange rate and/or reducing demand will require interest rates to be raised, possibly to extremely high levels.

Currency markets themselves intensify the instability of interest rates arising from the way monetary policy is conducted, and hence enlarge the interest rate risk for banks due to maturity mismatching of their assets and liabilities, particularly in international business. Variable-interest loans allow banks to pass through changes in funding costs to borrowers. However, these do not eliminate the risk but simply transform it into credit risk, as has been witnessed during the debt crisis. Moreover, such loans represent only a portion of total bank assets. The difficulty of matching perfectly the maturity structure of liabilities with the length of roll-over periods, which are, in general, fixed at certain intervals, increases the interest rate risk when interest rates are very volatile, especially since the maturity of liabilities tends to be shorter the more volatile interest rates are.

This shortening results naturally from the increased uncertainty created by the volatility of the financial environment and the increased liquidity preference of market participants. Financial instability tends to increase uncertainty and reduce the degree of confidence in the expectations held with respect to the future course of interest and exchange rates and security prices. Since uncertainty is the essence of liquidity preference, as uncertainty grows, liquidity preference increases. Not only are maturities shortened as the demand for capital-uncertain assets is reduced, but also interest rates, especially long-term rates, are pushed up to cover increased riskiness of interest-bearing financial assets.

There is evidence that this has indeed been happening. In the 1970s, as instability and uncertainty increased significantly alongside inflation, markets started to innovate to meet the increased demand for interest-bearing short-term assets, such as the negotiable order of withdrawal and the automatic transfer service accounts in the United States to bypass regulations regarding interest-rate ceilings on savings and demand deposits. Innovations have continued to burgeon, particularly in short-term liquid paper, in more recent years, even though inflation has been kept relatively low and stable. On the other hand, as will be seen below, interest rates stayed persistently high in the 1980s, particularly in the United States (and on dollar assets), where financial instability has been more pronounced than in other major countries. The increase in long-term interest rates in most countries has been greater, and these rates have been less sensitive to fluctuations in short-term rates compared to past decades.

Thus, the high interest rates experienced in recent years are due not only to the stance of monetary policy in major countries, which was, on average, tighter in the 1980s than in the past, but also to a number of systemic factors stemming from the asymmetry in international adjustment and exchange rate management and from the instability of the financial environment and of key financial prices.

Financial openness and policy autonomy

Increased financial openness and dismantling of barriers to capital flows have considerably strengthened the links among the financial markets of national economies. This has had significant implications for national policy autonomy and domestic and global effects of national economic policy. The degree of policy autonomy has declined everywhere, but most of all in smaller and/or less-developed countries having a high degree of financial openness. On the other hand, the global effects of the policies pursued by the major countries have increased considerably, even though their policy autonomy too has diminished.

Policy autonomy refers to the ability of national policy makers to control ultimate goals of policy—for example, the volume of output, the level of employment and the rate of inflation—by using the instruments at their disposal. The degree of policy autonomy or the effectiveness of national policy instruments in controlling ultimate goals depends on the strength of the influence of these instruments (directly or indirectly) on goals. It also depends on the stability of the link between instruments and goals and, hence, the predictability of the influence of the former on the latter. Financial openness reduces the degree of autonomy because it weakens the national policy influence on national goals and renders the link between national instruments and targets less reliable, making the relationship dependent on the behaviour of policy makers and markets elsewhere. Foreign policy action and economic shocks originating abroad exert significant constraints on the conduct of national policy and on its ability to attain policy goals.

Such cross-country influences are not usually known with a reasonable degree of accuracy. Knowledge about structural and behavioural relations that link the national economy to the rest of the world is very inadequate; available empirical models linking major countries differ both as regards the magnitude and the direction of cross-country policy influences. Moreover, access to information abroad is more difficult and costly, and developments in other countries are difficult to assess. An equally and perhaps more important source of uncertainty is the game-theoretic nature of decision-making by policy authorities in an interdependent world. What constitutes an appropriate policy action of a home government depends on what is assumed of the behaviour of foreign policy makers; but the latter, in turn, depends on assumptions about the policy course in the home economy. This not only creates problems in policy-making, but also can lead to serious conflicts when countries have incompatible objectives for exchange rates and trade balances.

Internationalization of finance and financial openness create increased possibilities for the private sector to circumvent various restrictions imposed by monetary authorities, such as credit ceilings and reserve requirements. Domestic monetary and credit aggregates become extremely difficult to define in a meaningful and useful way—that is, so as to provide reliable guidance for the conduct of monetary policy. For instance, there is no satisfactory and generally agreed way of dealing with the assets and liabilities of Eurobanks. Should a dollar deposit held in a London bank by a Colombian resident in Switzerland be included in the money supply of Colombia, the United States, the United Kingdom or Switzerland? The same question also arises with respect to credits from Eurobanks. It is very difficult to identify the influence of such deposits and credits on spending decisions in the various countries involved and thus to interpret movements in such aggregates in taking monetary policy action, particularly when monetary policy is targeting certain monetary and credit aggregates.

That increased financial interdependence leads to loss of policy effectiveness and autonomy for national governments does not imply that influences due to financial openness always undermine the achievement of policy objectives. That depends on the objectives pursued and on actions taken at home and abroad. For instance, in a financially open economy, fiscal stimulus tends to leak abroad because the consequent rise in interest rates encourages capital inflow, thereby appreciating the domestic currency and reducing net exports. By contrast, monetary tightening can lead to currency appreciation, which can reinforce the disinflationary impact of the monetary policy. Again, the ability to attract capital through financial policies can help to avoid taking deflationary action at times of serious external payments difficulties. However, in both cases there is a great deal of uncertainty as to the final outcome, not only because of the unpredictability of the response of international financial markets to such policy actions, but also because of their international repercussions and the policy response of foreign Governments. This uncertainty and the associated costs of loss of control over national economies can only be reduced by collective action, involving management of international money and finance and of interdependence.

For a developing country, financial openness would bring an even greater loss of policy autonomy. For one thing, the country would be unable to de-link its real interest rates from those abroad. Indeed, domestic real interest rates would be pushed well above the levels prevailing in world markets, particularly where there is macroeconomic instability and a persistent external debt problem.

Moreover, the link between exchange and interest rates can be much more destabilizing in developing countries. A major industrial country may be able to influence its exchange rate by monetary policy actions regardless of the state of its external balances. In developing countries, however, exchange rates are influenced to a much greater extent by external payments. This means that payments disturbances tend to feed into domestic interest rates, for competition with foreign assets requires that domestic interest rates should cover interest rates on foreign assets plus the expected rate of depreciation of the currency. When the currency is expected to depreciate in real terms, domestic real interest rates would be raised further. This link can pose serious problems for fiscal and monetary management, particularly where the public sector needs to borrow in domestic markets in order to service its external debt, as has been observed in many countries in recent years.

C
FINANCIAL AND CURRENCY MARKETS IN THE 1980s

Developments in world currency and financial markets in the 1980s clearly illustrate various types of destabilizing interactions among monetary policy, interest rates, securities prices and exchange rates described in the previous section. Indeed, world financial and currency markets were more unstable than in the 1970s, even though real economic activity in the major developed market economies showed a considerable degree of stability.

Monetary policy and interest rates

During the past decade, interest rates in the major reserve currency countries were both extremely high by historical standards and highly unstable. In the 1980s, short-term interest rate instability was no lower than in the 1970s and markedly higher than in the years before the advent of floating exchange rates. Interest rate variability increased substantially in all the major currency countries during the period of disinflation in the early 1980s; compared to the 1960s, it had doubled in Japan, the United Kingdom and France and increased more than five times in the United States. Since 1982, interest rate instability has been lower than in the 1960s in the Federal Republic of Germany, but it has remained particularly high in the United States and the United Kingdom.

The uncertainty ruling financial markets also becomes evident when account is taken of the fact that alterations in the direction of movements in interest rates have been more frequent than at any other time since the war, including in Japan and the Federal Republic of Germany. In addition to increased short-term (weekly or monthly) instability, there were two periods in the 1980s during which interest rates underwent substantial swings in all the major currency countries: in the early 1980s, when monetary policy was geared to disinflation; and during 1987–1989, when the focus of monetary policy shifted back and forth between currency and financial markets and, particularly in the United States, between fears of recession and inflation. During the latter period there were also substantial swings in share prices, to an extent unprecedented in the post-war period.

Interest rates in the major reserve currency countries, in particular in the United States and the United Kingdom, were also higher in the past decade than previously. Short-term nominal rates were, on average, also high in the 1970s, but so was inflation: in real terms, with the exception of the Federal Republic of Germany, they were negative. After 1981, as inflation eased, nominal rates began to fall from their peak of 1980–1981. But, generally, they did not fall significantly below the average level of the 1970s, although inflation declined considerably. Consequently, real interest rates increased strongly compared to the previous decade and also exceeded those of the more stable 1960s by between one half (Federal Republic of Germany) and more than four times (United Kingdom).

This generalized increase in interest rates is primarily due to the fact that monetary policy has been, on average, tighter. However, as already noted, increased instability and uncertainty have also influenced the level and term structure of interest rates. It is noteworthy that, comparing the 1980s with the 1960s, in the United States long-term interest rates have increased much more than short-term rates. This steepening of the yield curve cannot be explained by expectations of an acceleration of inflation; inflation has not only been falling since the early 1980s, but it has been lower, on average, than in the 1960s. These factors could have been expected to push future short-term interest rates below the current rates. The steepening of the yield curve in the 1980s, together with the proliferation of holdings of liquid short-term assets, suggests that the increased instability of interest rates and the exchange rate of the dollar has been an important factor in the increase in interest rates, one which can also help explain the evidence that the ability of the term structure of interest rates to forecast future inflation is very much limited.

Three basic factors account for the increased financial instability of the 1980s. First, a fundamental change took place in the conduct of monetary policy, away from targeting interest rates. Secondly, financial deregulation allowed markets greater scope to innovate and generate disturbances, thereby reducing the capacity of central banks to achieve their objectives. Thirdly, as will be discussed below, monetary policy became overloaded as Governments tried to manage exchange rates without coordinating their macroeconomic and, particularly, their fiscal policies. The pressures in exchange markets tended to be propagated to equity markets through their effects on monetary policy and interest rates; but when equity prices fell precipitously, monetary policy had to be redirected once again.

In the 1960s and the 1970s, monetary policy was generally aimed at keeping interest rates low and stable with a view to providing a favourable financial environment for productive investment. This was helped in many countries by the widespread practice of direct regulation of interest rates. Monetary policy was discretionary and shared the task of short-term demand management with fiscal and, to some extent, price and income policies. In the late 1970s and early 1980s, many central banks switched to quantitative targets for certain monetary aggregates and embarked upon a strict disinflationary policy stance. During this phase, both the level and the instability of nominal interest rates reached new peaks, particularly in the United States. This happened not only because interest rates are inevitably more unstable under the operating procedure chosen, but also because the assumptions underlying this monetarist approach proved wrong, resulting not only in a substantially increased instability in the financial system, but also in a deflationary overkill.

Strict monetarism in the conduct of monetary policy was abandoned in the United States at the end of 1982, when it was recognized that financial deregulation and innovation had significantly reduced the control of the Federal Reserve over certain monetary aggregates and that inflation was not as closely governed by monetary aggregates as had been assumed. Money supply targeting has continued, though with broader definitions of money, wide target ranges and the use of a number of indicators, including interest rates, in the conduct of monetary policy. The new operating regime has tended to result in less pronounced short-term fluctuations in interest rates than strict monetarism, but greater instability than a regime of interest rate targeting.

Exchange rates and financial markets

The exchange rates of the major currencies in the 1980s were much more unstable than their interest rates; short-term instability intensified at the beginning of the 1980s and showed no tendency to diminish in subsequent years. Bilateral exchange rates among the United States dollar, Japanese yen and Deutsche mark have been particularly volatile. By contrast, since the inception of the European Monetary System, bilateral exchange rates among member currencies have, on average, fluctuated much less.

More important are the longer-term swings in key exchange rates which lasted for several years. The real effective exchange rate of the dollar rose by more than 40 per cent between 1980 and mid-1984, remained there for about a year and then fell back below the level of 1980 within a matter of about two years. The Japanese yen, in turn, moved up in real terms by more than 35 per cent between early 1985 and November 1988, but fell by around 20 per cent between that date and March 1990.

The behaviour of exchange rates in the 1980s cannot be systematically explained by the variables generally cited as their determinants— that is, interest rates, price levels and trade and current account balances; empirical models seeking to do so have failed. These variables, and the macroeconomic policies that exert a strong influence on them, do influence the demand for foreign exchange, but their impact on exchange rates is not systematic or predictable. Because of the speculative nature of currency markets, the influence of the variables cited depends on whether or not they have been anticipated and on how they affect expectations regarding the future course of exchange rates. Moreover, for the same reason, expectations regarding the future course of exchange rates can change and alter the current pattern of exchange rates independently of macroeconomic policy; in other words, speculative bubbles occur whereby a currency appreciates simply because investors believe that it will go even higher in the future.

In some periods, exchange rates have moved in line with current account developments because the latter were expected to trigger monetary policy actions that would influence the future course of exchange rates. For instance, in 1987 and early 1988, announcements of United States monthly trade figures caused strong reactions on foreign exchange markets. But the widening of trade imbalances among the major OECD countries in the first half of the 1980s did not influence the dollar until 1985, when they had grown so big as to give rise to expectations that policy actions would be taken to avert the resulting tensions in the trading system. Similarly, in certain periods, the dollar's exchange rates against other major reserve currencies moved in line with current short-term interest differentials, but there have also been a number of episodes when the relationship was inversed.

As well as increased difficulties in predicting the future course of monetary policy, one of the factors increasing the volatility of market sentiment, and thus adding substantially to both the short-term variability of exchange rates and, more important, the medium-term swings, has been inconsistencies in the fiscal and monetary policies of the major OECD countries. The expansionary fiscal and restrictive monetary policies pursued by the United States, at a time when the overall stance of policies in the other major OECD countries was contractionary, was a major factor in the appreciation of the dollar in the early 1980s; this, together with disparities in the pace of domestic demand in the United States and its major trading partners, was the most important reason for the huge United States trade deficit. Most major OECD countries, however, chose to ignore these developments for almost half a decade.

The Plaza meeting, held in New York in September 1985, marked for most Governments a major reassessment of the roles to be assigned to markets and public policy in the determination of exchange rates. It marked the beginning of exchange rate management which played a major role in correcting the misalignment of the dollar until the Louvre meeting, held in Paris in February 1987. However, the Plaza agreement emphasized primarily intervention in exchange markets. The dollar had already begun to decline before this date, and it was believed that coordinated intervention and monetary measures were needed to bring about further devaluation thought necessary for adjustment; but there was no general agreement on the need for expansionary fiscal policy outside the United States.

At first, this did not prove troublesome, as monetary policy actions were "leaning with the wind". However, the exchange rate mechanism proved much less effective than expected in correcting payments imbalances, given the pattern of demand generation. At the Louvre meeting consensus was reached among the governments of the Group of Seven that the dollar should be stabilized and that the adjustment in trade balances should be achieved through enhanced coordination of macroeconomic policies among the participating countries, directed at changing the international pattern of domestic demand; the actions taken in pursuit of this objective were to include fiscal policies. This implied a restrictive monetary policy and budget cuts on the part of the United States and the pursuit of more expansionary management of domestic demand, partly through a stronger fiscal stimulus, on the part of the Federal Republic of Germany and Japan. Thus, it was broadly agreed that the trade adjustment required was not attainable solely through exchange rate management.

During the period from February to September 1987, there was a degree of exchange rate stability unprecedented during the decade. The orderly decline in the dollar attained between the Plaza and Louvre meetings, and the subsequent success in keeping the dollar stable, gave impetus to new initiatives to manage exchange rates in the OECD area. The reasons for this move towards managed floating were clearly expressed by the British Chancellor of the Exchequer at the annual meetings of the International Monetary Fund and the World Bank in September 1987: "The belief that markets would provide a stabilizing influence, through the operations of medium-term speculators, has not been borne out. . . In particular, we have seen wild gyrations in the dollar that have clearly not been a reflection of economic fundamentals. . . Moreover, these gyrations have damaged growth in world trade.
. . And the major uncertainties about exchange rate movements inhibited risk-taking and required a switching of resources at a pace that was totally unrealistic." He added that the regime of managed floating adopted at the Louvre meeting has worked because countries have "been prepared in practice to give significant weight to exchange rates

in the conduct of monetary policy . . . and to back up (the) agreement with coordinated intervention" and that the experience gained should be used "to build up a more permanent regime of managed floating".

However, the exchange rate stability between February and September 1987 was attained at the cost of increased pressures on monetary policy. The Louvre agreement was translated only partly into actual measures, the United States trade deficit failed to improve and, consequently, pressures on the dollar intensified. Heavy intervention in foreign exchange markets by the United States, the Federal Republic of Germany and Japan was therefore required. Thus, monetary policy had to bear the brunt of adjustment and soon became overburdened. Intervention and the consequent monetary expansion by surplus countries gave rise to concerns that exchange rate management would undermine their efforts to maintain price stability and contain inflationary expectations. As a result, monetary policy was tightened in the course of the year, causing interest rates in the major OECD countries to rise.

This created a situation of fragility in financial markets. Rising long-term bond yields were accompanied by falling dividend yields; in the three major stock markets, increases in share prices pushed the price-earnings ratios to record levels. On the other hand, the failure of the depreciation of the dollar to significantly improve the United States trade deficit gave rise to concerns that interest rates in the United States might have to be raised further to stem downward pressures on the dollar. Fears that such developments would cause a drop in activity and profitability triggered the collapse of stock prices in October 1987.

This collapse induced monetary authorities, particularly in the United States, temporarily to put aside other objectives and provide the financial markets with additional liquidity. This succeeded in its objective of containing financial market turbulence and in avoiding a recession, but it also meant a relaxation of exchange rate management. As the perception of an inflationary danger mounted, the choice between exchange rate and domestic stability in deficit countries came increasingly to be decided in favour of the latter. Thus, monetary policy tightened again in the course of 1988 and interest rates were pushed even higher than before the crash.

A similar situation also evolved in the course of 1989. In October 1989, the second largest day-to-day fall in the Dow Jones index was recorded, and again this was closely related to exchange rate pressures and monetary policy. The dollar had been rising when the United States trade deficit increased unexpectedly in October 1989, generating uncertainties about future macroeconomic policies and interest rates. Bringing down the external deficit through currency depreciation would have required United States interest rates to be lowered, but that was considered inimical to domestic price stability; alternatively, reducing imports through cuts in domestic demand via monetary restraint would have implied higher interest rates and depressed corporate profits.

Finally, the behaviour of the Tokyo Stock Exchange during early 1990 generated similar destabilizing feedbacks between currency and financial markets, and policies failed to block their propagation. The Tokyo Stock Exchange was not affected by the "mini-crash" of 1989 in the United States and the Federal Republic of Germany, but continued to boom, reaching a new peak at the end of that year. However, during the subsequent four months, the Nikkei index dropped by about 25 per cent (steeper though slower than the drop in the Dow Jones in October 1987), government bonds by more than 20 per cent and the yen by over 10 per cent. These changes were interrelated. As fears of recession in the United States subsided and inflation became the primary concern of monetary policy, interest rates tended to rise. This, in combination with the policy of low interest rates in Japan and the expectation of higher rates in the Federal Republic of Germany (prompted mainly by developments in Eastern Europe), exerted substantial downward pressure on the yen and triggered massive shifts from yen-denominated assets, which accentuated the downward pressures on the value of the yen and also brought down bond and equity prices. The central banks of the other major countries gave only limited support to the yen. This created a dilemma for Japan, similar to that faced by the

United States in 1987; higher interest rates were needed to stabilize the currency, but these could further destabilize the equity market. Moreover, the continued decline of the yen triggered expectations of substantial increases in domestic interest rates, which fed into further declines in bond and equity prices. Eventually, interest rates had to be raised, with the discount rate reaching double the level of mid-1989.

These episodes illustrate the point that interactions among financial and currency markets tend to be destabilizing and that monetary policy cannot easily deal with them simultaneously. Monetary policy has had to shift from one objective to another, as actions taken to ensure stability in one market have destabilized others. These shifts have tended to make the future course of key financial prices more unpredictable and uncertain. Moreover, because the burden of adjustment has generally been on weak-currency and/or deficit countries, efforts to manage exchange rates have tended to push up interest rates.

The enthusiasm regarding exchange rate management faded away with the 1987 stock market crash, brought about because, as noted above, there was an unwillingness, particularly in the United States and the Federal Republic of Germany, to make the necessary fiscal policy adjustments. Immediately after the crisis, exchange rate instability rose again, as monetary policy was focused first on the stability of the financial system and then on internal objectives, in particular, the price level. Foreign exchange market intervention was reduced and monetary policy largely lost view of exchange rates.

There can be little doubt that there is now an increased awareness by policy makers that action is needed to attenuate instability. Thus, these shifts of direction in the conduct of monetary policy simply reflect the major dilemmas that the policy makers are facing, namely, too few policy instruments to attain many objectives simultaneously in an environment characterized by increased volatility of markets and continued failure to coordinate policies in order to manage exchange rates and reduce trade imbalances.

D
STRENGTHENING THE INTERNATIONAL MONETARY SYSTEM

The adverse consequences of the increased instability of the international monetary and financial system are not always fully appreciated, in large part because visible and significant damage to the real economy of developed countries has so far been averted. However, the experience of the past decade shows that financial instability and disruption are costly not only potentially but also in fact. Moreover, the incidence of these costs does not always fall on countries and sectors whose actions contribute most to instability. Developing countries are particularly vulnerable to financial disruption and exchange rate disorder, as amply illustrated by the experience of the 1980s.

The adverse effects of instability on growth and development work primarily through debt, investment and trade and flow from three sources: first, there is a systemic bias towards higher rates of interest; secondly, exchange rates are de-linked from the fundamentals of the real economy; and thirdly, both interest rates and, particularly, exchange rates tend to move excessively and unpredictably.

The stock of external debt of developing countries is the most important channel of transmission of disruption and instability in world financial and currency markets into their domestic economies. Thus, the absence of a tendency for equalization of rates of return on assets denominated in different currencies means that the cost of servicing debt depends crucially on its currency composition and is influenced not only by changes in the overall level of interest rates, but also by changes in exchange rates. This causes serious problems in the management of debt and can give rise to significant losses when there is a mismatch between the currency composition of debt and foreign exchange receipts and reserves. On the other hand, since most developing countries do not have unlimited access to each of the major international capital markets, they cannot easily adjust the currency composition of their external debt or take forward cover to alleviate the effects of financial and currency market disturbances.

There can be little doubt that the systemic tendency of interest rates to remain high was an important factor in the debt crisis of the 1980s. Its effects on developing countries were aggravated because a large stock of debt had already been built up before this tendency emerged in force; interest rate increases were passed on to the debtors via the variable-interest loan practice, and rates of return on real domestic assets in debtor countries were depressed by deflationary adjustments, mainly because of investment cuts.

The tendency of interest rates to stay high depresses investment permanently unless the increase in the cost of finance is offset by reductions in other costs. Declines in real unit labour and material costs in the major industrial countries in the 1980s helped first to stem and then to reverse the downward trend in rates of profits, raising them by the end of the decade to the levels of the late 1960s and early 1970s. However, this has been attained at the cost of a substantial rise in unemployment and a fall in commodity prices. Since real interest rates remain, on average, much higher than in the 1960s, profit rates characteristic of the 1960s may not translate into investment rates experienced during that period. Indeed, despite recent increases, the share of investment in GDP in the Group of Seven countries remains below the level of the late 1960s and early 1970s.

Given the present and prospective stance of fiscal policies, the degree of monetary relaxation needed to bring interest rates down to levels conducive to a rapid pace of capital accumulation is likely to be regarded as too expansionary by many central bankers. At the same time, systematically high interest rates place monetary policy on a tightrope. Should there be a supply shock on prices, for example, policy makers would be faced with the unattractive option of either tightening policy, allowing interest rates to shoot up from already high levels, thereby virtually ensuring recession, or allowing prices to feed through, thereby creating a ratcheting upward of rates of inflation. While this dilemma is always present, the higher the interest rates to begin with, the more acutely it is felt.

Investment is hindered also by increased instability of exchange rates. Unpredictable swings in exchange rates tend to deter investment in the tradeable goods sector because of uncertainty as regards profitability, for, once in place, production capacity cannot be redeployed from one industry to another without incurring substantial costs. Moreover, increased unpredictability of exchange rates distorts the spatial allocation of foreign direct investment, which tends to be governed by the desire to reduce the exchange rate risk rather than by considerations of efficiency.

Exchange rate volatility also increases the risk and uncertainty in international trade and depresses exports and imports; this happens even when risks are covered in forward markets because of the costs involved. Indeed, many studies indicate that exchange rate fluctuations have had significant adverse effects on trade for a number of both developed and developing countries, in large part because of increased costs on the demand and supply sides.

More important, exchange rate misalignments tend to disrupt the international trading system by triggering protectionism. Overvaluation of currencies gives rise to protectionist pressures and, ultimately, to protectionist measures which are not removed when misalignment is corrected; often permanent protection is sought in order to compensate for long-term exposure to exchange rate risk. Similarly, currency undervaluation can lead to investment in industries which are otherwise uncompetitive; again, such industries could exert substantial pressure for protection when the exchange rate misalignment is corrected. Evidence strongly suggests that these effects played a major role in the proliferation of non-tariff barriers in the 1980s.

These and other adverse consequences of instability, as well as the susceptibility of the financial system to crisis, necessitate actions designed to attain a more stable system of international money and finance. The previous sections show that while the factors that generate disturbances and disruption are several and complex and it is not always easy to assess accurately their relative importance, action will be needed simultaneously on two broad fronts, namely, markets and policies. The next section briefly discusses possible ways of improving the functioning of markets and the design and mutual compatibility of policies in the major OECD countries.

Regulation and supervision of finance and capital flows

Given the degree of development of the organization of financial markets and the increased predominance of speculative activities, it is not altogether clear that an appropriate design of policies both within and among the major OECD countries would be sufficient to avert financial disruptions and destabilizing capital flows. Consequently, there is a need to give serious consideration to possible ways and means of reducing the scope of markets to generate disruption and instability without undermining their ability to facilitate the proper allocation of savings. In this respect, two main questions arise: is regulation necessary to ensure stability, and does regulation undermine efficiency.

Answers to these questions will clearly be shaped, *inter alia,* by the type of regulation being considered. In this respect, a distinction can be made among three categories: (a) prudential regulations designed to limit the risk taken by financial institutions—for example, capital adequacy, liquidity requirements and diversification rules; (b) protective regulations designed to shelter investors, particularly depositors at commercial banks—for example, deposit insurance and lender-of-last-resort facilities; and (c) what may be called "systemic (or macroprudential) regulations", designed primarily to reduce systemic disturbances and instability. Clearly, both prudential and protective regulations also serve this purpose, but their focus is more on specific institutions and investors. Among the types of measures included in systemic regulations are various controls and restrictions on capital movements, as well as taxation designed to discourage speculation.

Under conditions in which interest rates are fully deregulated and restrictions are significantly eased on access to financial markets and types of transactions permitted, the importance of having an effective system of prudential regulations is considerably enhanced. However, in the 1980s the tendency was to broaden protective regulations, through deposit insurance or *ex post* financial rescue operations, without matching this with prudential regulation. This created a moral hazard problem and played a major role in financial disruptions in certain countries—for example, savings and loan associations in the United States. There is now an increased consensus concerning the need for vigorous prudential regulations to avoid such disruptions, at least for financial intermediaries.

Prudential regulations often trigger innovations by markets to avoid them, and, with increased financial openness, such reactions tend to gravitate more to the international than to the national level. Recent efforts to harmonize the regulatory regimes for the financial systems of different countries reflect awareness of this tendency. An important reason for improving international cooperation in the area of banking supervision is that differences in national regulatory regimes can generate international financial transactions with little or no underlying economic justification. Various evidence indicates that large capital movements frequently take place solely with the aim of circumventing monetary regulations such as minimum reserve requirements, prudential controls regarding capital adequacy and liquidity, and restrictions and rules concerning foreign exchange transactions. Moreover, during periods when confidence is adversely affected by financial turbulence, large movements of funds may be triggered from financial centres perceived as "soft" to safer havens, principally the major financial markets in the OECD area. Thus, the Basel Agreement of July 1988 among the central bank governors of the Group of Ten countries and Luxembourg concerning a common, risk-based standard of capital adequacy for international banks constitutes a useful step in the process of reducing the incentive to international capital movements associated with divergences in national regulatory regimes.

Since such agreements concerning prudential regulations do not cover offshore centres, they may encourage further relocation of banking activities. This, in fact, happened in the 1960s and 1970s and subsequently triggered competitive deregulation in the major money and capital market countries. The need for effective prudential regulation is now increasingly recognized, but unless the regulatory regime becomes truly international, differential regulatory and tax treatment may continue to shift activity to offshore centres.

Moreover, there are serious gaps in preventive regulations even at the national level. Many countries do not have adequate and effective safeguards against the assumption of excessive risks in securities markets. Thus, during the 1980s there was increased proliferation of high-risk debt instruments, such as junk bonds in the United States, used primarily for corporate take-overs. Absence of prudential regulations in such areas has also encouraged regulated institutions to enter into such transactions via off-balance-sheet business.

While it is widely recognized that financial and currency markets have become increasingly speculative, the issue of restrictions on short-term capital movements remains highly controversial. The resistance to such measures is based on two premises: that they will not be effective; and that they tend to result in inefficiencies in the allocation of resources internationally because it is not possible to separate speculative flows from those that respond to fundamentals.

There can be little doubt that restrictions on capital flows can be ineffective and even counter-productive if they are used as substitutes for exchange rate alignment and/or policy adjustment. However, as stressed above, regulations and restrictions regarding financial transactions and flows would need to complement appropriate policies, rather than be a substitute for them, and would be used solely for the purpose of reducing the scope of markets to create and propagate disturbances.

On the other hand, there are forms of regulations, other than quantitative and administrative controls, that work primarily via the price mechanism and that help to deter short-term, as opposed to long-term, capital movements. An example of such a measure is the interest equalization tax which was used in the past before the advent of floating. Another measure available for the purpose is the application to foreign exchange markets of the tax on financial transactions originally proposed by Keynes:

> "It is usually agreed that casinos should, in the public interest, be inaccessible and expensive. And perhaps the same is true of Stock Exchanges. That the sins of the London Stock Exchange are less than those of Wall Street may be due, not so much to differences in national character, as to the fact that to the average Englishman Throgmorton Street is, compared with Wall Street to the average American, inaccessible and very expensive. The jobber's 'turn', the high brokerage charges and the heavy transfer tax payable to the Exchequer, which attend dealings on the London Stock Exchange, sufficiently diminish the liquidity of the market . . . to rule out a large proportion of the transactions characteristic of Wall Street. The introduction of a substantial government transfer tax on all transactions might prove the most serviceable reform available, with a view to mitigating the predominance of speculation over enterprise in the United States."[3]

Such a tax, to be effective, should be an internationally agreed uniform tax, applied in proportion to the size of transactions involving conversions of one currency into another in order to raise the cost of short-run transactions relative to longer-run currency conversions and maturities. Such an agreement would be of unprecedented scope. Its benefits, however, would be fully commensurate with the effort required.

Exchange rate arrangements

There is now widespread recognition that the floating exchange rate system has failed to promote stable and sustainable current account balances and that there is a need to move to a more stable system of exchange rates. Such a system should be sufficiently flexible to allow exchange rates to adjust to underlying economic conditions, in particular to changes in prices and productivity and, hence, to avoid the mistakes of the Bretton Woods regime. It should also avoid the mistakes of the last two decades.

One of the arguments in favour of floating exchange rates was that they would give countries autonomy and independence in domestic policy-making. The autonomy in question was partly with respect to monetary policy: since there would be no obligation to defend a particular exchange rate, monetary policy would have greater scope to deal with domestic objectives. However, as discussed above, this has proved rather illusory because of increased financial integration of the countries and increased instability of exchange rates. It is no longer possible to ignore the consequences of exchange rates for domestic policy objectives and to pursue an autonomous monetary policy.

A broader issue of policy autonomy is related to trade adjustment. It was implicitly, and sometimes explicitly, assumed that external equilibrium could be attained primarily through movements in exchange rates, rather than in domestic demand and income, thereby allowing countries to pursue macroeconomic policies geared to full employment and growth. This expectation was based on two premises: first, that there would be no major shortcomings in the conduct of policies both within and across the countries; and, secondly, that trade balances would respond swiftly to changes in exchange rates. However, as recent experience has shown, both of these assumptions have proved to be wrong.

There can be little doubt that no exchange rate system can work efficiently when there are serious macroeconomic policy shortcomings. As the experience of the United States has demonstrated, inconsistency in the mix of monetary and fiscal policies can cause exchange rate movements that aggravate trade imbalances. On the other hand, when trade imbalances are due primarily to major divergences between the overall stances of the macroeconomic policies of the major trading partners, and/or because trade policy is significantly restrictive in some of these countries, attempts to reduce trade imbalances through exchange rate movements would entail sharp swings in exchange rates; or, should exchange rates come under pressure, attempts to stabilize them could cause serious strains.

Regarding the second assumption of the floating system, recent experience has also shown that the response of exports and imports to exchange rates can be very sluggish. Markets for traded goods do not necessarily operate on the basis of the type of competitive pricing envisaged by the proponents of floating exchange rates. In particular, greater instability of exchange rates raises the average profit margin. The latter also becomes much more variable in order to allow prices to be adjusted to changes in exchange rates, thereby rendering exchange rate movements much less effective in correcting trade imbalances. The sharp depreciation of the dollar since early 1985 brought about much less improvement in trade imbalances among the major OECD countries than had been expected because exporters preferred to take cuts in their profit margins rather than reduce export volumes and lose their share of the United States market, whereas United States producers tended to respond to the dollar depreciation not so much by raising their export volumes as their profit margins.

These considerations show that the scope for attaining a stable pattern of exchange rates will depend, *inter alia,* on the degree of consistency of policies within and between the major countries. However, experience has shown that the discipline needed to eliminate policy inconsistencies is hard to obtain without effective multilateral surveillance, an issue that will be taken up in the following subsection.

The second important issue in the management of exchange rates is the need for an international commitment by the major OECD countries to an explicitly announced pattern of exchange rates that is compatible with underlying fundamentals, and to defend it by intervention in currency markets and regulation and control of financial flows. Such commitments would play an important role in achieving stability by providing an anchor for expectations, thereby influencing market behaviour, and by disciplining policy making.

The experience with exchange rate management by the Group of Ten countries after the Louvre meeting—the so-called reference ranges—constituted a direct targeting of exchange rates without, however, containing some of the above elements needed for durable stability. The ranges were not announced explicitly; they were agreed provisionally with a view to short-term adjustment needs and not because they reflected fundamentals; there were no formal obligations and rules in the event of the divergence of the rates from the agreed reference ranges; and, more important, the agreement did not secure policy adjustments needed to reduce pressures on exchange rates.

Lack of a firm commitment to defend the agreed pattern of exchange rates is also a feature of a version of the target zones proposal which favours "soft margins" in order to allow considerable flexibility and facilitate exchange rate management. Wide margins—for example, plus and minus 10 per cent—are advocated, *inter alia,* in order to absorb certain temporary shocks within the zones and because of substantial uncertainty in calculating the appropriate pattern of exchange rates. However, wide margins make sense only if there is a commitment to defending the targets. Moreover, it is not clear if such a system can ensure the discipline needed and thereby be regarded as credible by the markets.

Since a firm commitment among participating Governments is essential for achieving greater exchange rate stability, and since reduction of unsustainable trade imbalances should rely more on adjustment in policies in both deficit and surplus countries than on exchange rates, the question arises as to whether an adjustable peg system with predefined obligations and narrow ranges along the lines of the European Monetary System would be feasible. Such a system, in combination with regulation and control of short-term capital flows discussed above, would leave much less room for speculative pressures and policy inconsistencies to build up and could thus be more successful in preventing the emergence of misalignments. However, like other proposals for reference ranges and target zones, it would require not only agreed intervention rules but also a framework within which national monetary and fiscal policies would have to be conducted and coordinated.

Interdependence, policy coordination and surveillance

Since exchange rate instability is undesirable because of the adverse effects of unpredictable and misaligned exchange rates on growth and development, it is essential that a system designed to attain exchange rate stability does not contain a deflationary bias. This clearly raises the question of assigning responsibilities and obligations to defend exchange rates and to undertake policy adjustment in order to correct destabilizing and unsustainable trade imbalances. Indeed, it evokes the whole question of the management of interdependence, which has become the central concept in recent discussions of policy coordination among the major OECD countries. However, actions have not always reflected its true meaning and policy implications.

Interdependence among countries implies that the economy of each is both sufficiently open for it to come under considerable influence from abroad and sufficiently large for its own policies to make a significant impact on others.

Appropriate management of interdependence implies that no country with a sufficiently open economy—even if it is too small to have itself an impact on other economies—should be expected to be able to put its house in order regardless of what the other countries are doing. Otherwise, the burden of adjustment would be put on deficit countries, thereby introducing a global deflationary bias. Nor should any country set its policies without paying attention to their possible international consequences, an approach that would lead to beggar-my-neighbour policies designed to export unemployment or inflation, thereby creating considerable friction in the international monetary and trading systems. The experience of the 1980s leading to the emergence of serious exchange rate misalignments and large trade imbalances, and to the subsequent failure to reduce them and to manage exchange rates, shows that the major OECD countries have been unable to take proper account of interdependence and to coordinate their macroeconomic policies accordingly.

Effective policy coordination necessitates agreement on certain goals and on policy actions needed when outcomes differ from the agreed goals. First, certain objectives need to be set for each country concerned, including admissible rates of growth of domestic demand, as well as exchange rates and current account balances. Consistency of objectives needs to be attained both within and between the countries concerned. It is particularly important to secure a pattern of demand generation consistent with trade and exchange rate objectives; and the latter need to be mutually consistent among the countries, since the number of exchange rates or current account balances that can serve as independent targets is less than the number of countries. There should be a clear understanding about the allocation of the burden of adjustment when the outcomes persistently deviate from the agreed targets.

Secondly, a set of global targets and indicators may be used to prevent a deflationary or inflationary bias in the overall policy stance and to provide a basis for global action by all the countries concerned. A recent proposal in this respect is that of introducing a commodity price index as an indicator to help monitor the performance of the group of industrial countries as a whole and to serve as an early-warning signal of potential price trends. This proposal is based on the assumption that global demand pressures are reflected in movements in commodity prices; indeed, deflationary policies played a major role in the collapse of commodity prices in the 1980s. Since they still remain depressed, an important issue is the level to be taken as the basis for assessment of their future movements.

Coordination of policies within such a framework does not necessarily imply automatic policy reactions to developments in certain indicators. A considerable amount of flexibility and discretion may be introduced, based on extensive consultations among the parties concerned. However, it should also be recognized that it necessarily implies a certain degree of constraint on national policy-making.

There can be little doubt that there are serious difficulties in attaining the required degree of coordination. Experience shows that coordination has been more successful when collective goals were pursued, such as the adjustment to the oil price rises in the 1970s, but it is not always possible to reach agreement on such goals. Often, policy coordination is required where the precise nature and causes of problems affecting several countries do not command consensus. In the present situation, for instance, the problem of trade imbalances is perceived differently by different countries. Moreover, there may be considerable differences in priorities attached to different ultimate goals by different countries. For example, views as to what is sustainable in terms of output growth can differ according to perceptions regarding trade-offs with environmental objectives. Another major difficulty is that the contribution of a national government to international economic cooperation carries little weight in the formation of voters' opinion, and the policy record of a government usually takes little account of external influences on the home economy. A basic requirement to overcome such difficulties is that policy makers and electorates in the major OECD countries understand that the international orientation of macroeconomic policy is a necessity stemming from interdependence that the very same countries have been promoting by advocating more liberal policies and open economies; nor is it against their own country's interest, since the alternative would be serious disruptions to national and global economies.

Policy coordination among the major countries would also need to take into account its implications for small but open economies and, particularly, for developing countries. As experience has demonstrated, these countries are affected not only by the overall stance of macroeconomic policies in the major OECD countries, which exerts a major influence on their volume and terms of trade, but even by the mix of monetary and fiscal policies which, through its effects on interest rates, has a major influence on their external debt burden. This is perhaps one of the most important reasons why the conduct of policies in the major countries should be subject to multilateral surveillance.

The record in this respect is extremely poor. Increased interdependence among the major OECD countries, increased dependence of economic performance in developing countries on the mix and stance of policies in the major OECD countries, and the greatly enhanced capacity of financial markets and capital flows to generate global disturbances mean that the world economy today is considerably different from the one envisaged by the architects of the post-war monetary arrangements. This would have required the strengthening of the surveillance function of the International Monetary Fund in order to help attain the objectives of growth and stability as laid down in article I of its Articles of Agreement. Instead, the last two decades have seen a considerable strengthening of the Fund's position *vis-à-vis* the developing countries, while issues of great importance to the global economy have continued to be decided within the Group of Five or the Group of Seven countries.

The inadequacy of IMF surveillance is now widely recognized. The Group of Ten countries, for instance, agreed that surveillance had not been as effective as was desirable in influencing national policies and promoting underlying economic conditions conducive to exchange rate stability, and they noted that some countries appeared to have been able on occasion to sustain policy courses not fully compatible with the goals of international adjustment and financial stability. The Group of Twenty-Four has argued that surveillance should not be limited to members' exchange rate policies, but should also include the international adjustment process. There is broad agreement that effective surveillance requires assessment of all policies affecting trade, capital flows, external adjustment and the effective functioning of the international monetary system, particularly of the major OECD countries.

The IMF has so far developed a number of medium-term economic indicators and has used them primarily for periodic bilateral consultations with Governments. However, the surveillance function of the Fund has particular importance for the process of policy coordination itself; it should be conducted on a multilateral basis before issues regarding policies and indicators are taken up in bilateral consultations. In this way, it may help allocate the burden of adjustment between deficit and surplus countries and assure that coordination of macroeconomic policy in the major industrial countries leads to results for the world economy that are conducive to growth as well as stability.

Notes

1. John Maynard Keynes, *The General Theory of Employment, Interest and Money* (New York, Harcourt Brace and Co., 1935), pp.158, 159.

2. A. Lamfalussy, "The changing environment of central bank policy", in *American Economic Review. Papers and Proceedings,* May 1985, p. 411.

3. Keynes, *op. cit.,* pp. 159–160.

Chapter 6

THE INTERNATIONAL MONETARY SYSTEM IN PERSPECTIVE

Robert Solomon*

Today's international monetary arrangements are far different from what was expected, and conceived, at Bretton Woods 46 years ago.

The founding fathers at Bretton Woods—led by John Maynard Keynes and Harry White—designed a system in which exchange rates were pegged at "par values" and were altered only in the event of a "fundamental disequilibrium". While they did not define this term, part of what they had in mind was to prevent a repetition of the competitive depreciations of the 1930s. The exchange rate regime they established was expected to operate in conditions in which many of the member States of the International Monetary Fund (IMF)—and they focused their attention almost entirely on industrial countries—would continue to apply controls on international movements of private capital. The enormous increase in capital mobility and the globalization of capital markets that now characterize financial relationships among the industrial countries were not anticipated in 1944.

The problems of an international monetary system and its possible need for reform have traditionally been classified under three headings: adjustment, liquidity, and confidence. "Adjustment" means correction of

*Guest Scholar, the Brookings Institution, Washington, D.C.; Economist, Adviser and Director, Federal Reserve Board; former Vice-Chairman, Committee of Twenty.

large and persistent ("unsustainable") deficits and surpluses in balance-of-payments positions of countries; "liquidity" means the international reserves of countries; and "confidence" means stability in the holdings of international reserves. The system needs reform if it fails to provide for adjustment; if it permits the creation of an excess or a deficiency of official reserves; or if it does not prevent "runs on the bank" in the sense that private holders of currencies of certain countries seek to convert them massively into other currencies.

While the Bretton Woods agreement provided a rule of behaviour for exchange rates, it was surprisingly silent on rules for balance-of-payments adjustment. Keynes had tried to introduce some such rules, but his proposals were not accepted. As it turned out, the so-called adjustment process was asymmetrical under the Bretton Woods arrangements—that is, most of the burden of adjustment fell on countries in deficit; they faced the alternative of using up their reserves or imposing restrictive fiscal and monetary policies whether or not their economies were suffering from excess domestic demand.

Much attention was given to international liquidity—that is, reserve assets—under the old system. Gold played an important role as a reserve asset and as a settlement item between countries with a balance-of-payments deficit and those with a balance-of-payments surplus. The dollar was, already in 1944, a major reserve asset in what was called the gold-exchange standard; in that system, the United States Treasury stood ready to convert dollars into gold and gold into dollars for monetary authorities. It may be noted that, just as the Bretton Woods agreement did not spell out how countries were expected to act to "adjust" imbalances, it did not indicate how a growing world economy was to be supplied with growing reserves. Perhaps new gold production was expected to supply this need; it certainly did not. In the event, it was the United States balance of payments that, for better or worse, provided other countries with increasing foreign exchange reserves in the form of official dollar balances.

As to confidence, the United Kingdom experienced a number of sterling crises in the 1950s and 1960s, and in 1971 a dollar crisis led to the suspension of gold convertibility by the United States and eventually to the breakdown of the Bretton Woods system.

It is useful to take note of these deficiencies in the Bretton Woods system because a tendency exists among some observers to look back on it with nostalgia and to characterize present arrangements as a "non-system".

Existing international monetary arrangements

How can the present system be characterized with respect to the three criteria identified above?

With respect to adjustment, there is no question that sizeable payments imbalances are permitted to develop and persist. Among the seven largest industrial countries, for example, the average current account surplus or deficit as a proportion of GNP was 0.65 per cent from 1965 to 1970, 0.79 per cent from 1971 to 1980, and 2.0 per cent from 1981 to 1989; in the period 1985–1989, it was 2.6 per cent. In particular, the United States had a large current account deficit during most of the 1980s, while Germany and Japan had large surpluses. On the whole, these imbalances were financed smoothly. Except in 1987—when a substantial part of the United States deficit was covered by official capital flows as central banks abroad purchased dollars in an effort to prevent the dollar from depreciating relative mainly to the German mark and the Japanese yen—the United States deficit has tended to be overfinanced by private capital movements. This was so in the first half of the decade, when the dollar was appreciating steeply, and again in 1988–1989. The case can be made that it was not in the American interest for a large current account deficit to persist for so long and not in the interest of Japan and Germany to devote so large a fraction of their output to net exports, but it is doubtful that the international monetary system should be faulted for the existence and persistence of these imbalances. Since they were largely financed by private capital, even a gold standard would not have prevented them.

The present system also differs from the Bretton Woods blueprint in its arrangements for international liquidity. Today, gold plays virtually no role in the international monetary system, although the monetary authorities of many countries continue to hold it. Gold may now be regarded as part of the national patrimony, like the Louvre or the Prado, rather than as a monetary instrument. Today, most current account surpluses and deficits are financed by flows of private capital. Only rarely, as in 1987, do movements of official capital play a significant role in financing the current account surpluses and deficits of industrial countries.

Regarding confidence, there have been very few instances of instability in the composition of official reserves. Nor has the confidence of private holders of foreign assets been undermined, despite some forecasts of a "hard landing" and financial crises if the United States external deficit should persist.

These sanguine observations should not be taken to mean that all is for the best in the best of all possible international monetary systems. It is useful, therefore, to turn to the problems that beset the world economy today and to what sorts of reforms are desirable. But first it is necessary to take note of how the world has changed since the Bretton Woods system began to operate.

Increased interdependence

The Bretton Woods agreement was, in a way, a recognition of economic and financial interdependence, but that interdependence has intensified greatly in recent decades.

One aspect of greater interdependence is the degree of openness of economies to one another's trade. In the past 20 years, the volume of world trade has grown half again as fast as world output. For the seven largest industrial countries, this shows up as a 75 per cent increase in the ratio of merchandise trade to GNP since the mid-1950s. When account is taken of the fact that traded goods have risen less in price than other goods, the ratio of real exports and imports to real GNP is seen to have more than doubled since 1955.

The increased international mobility of capital, though a later development, has been even more dramatic. In the past 15 or 20 years, the dismantling of capital controls, the deregulation of financial markets and the application of computer technology have led to an enormous increase in capital flows among industrial countries. The computer has had two effects: it has made possible the creation of new financial instruments that facilitate flows of funds across national borders, and it has made new information available instantaneously throughout the world. As an illustration of the greater mobility of capital, between 1973 and 1989 deposits from abroad in the banks in industrial countries increased more than twelvefold, while aggregate deposits rose less than fivefold.

There are several consequences of enhanced interdependence. Two of them, both of which suggest possible reforms of the system, are identified here and elaborated later:

(a) Economies that are more open to each other in trade and finance are more affected by one another's policies and non-policy developments. This in turn provides the justification for closer coordination of economic policies;

(b) Exchange rates are subject to greater market pressures and show much greater volatility than in the past. Not only are day-to-day movements of exchange rates much larger, but also rates are subject to sizeable medium-term swings, sometimes including "overshooting". This has led to proposals for exchange rate reform. In Europe, members of the European Community, other than the United Kingdom, Greece and Portugal, adhere to the exchange rate mechanism of the European Monetary System and keep their rates within margins of 2.25 per cent of one another's central rates, which are readjusted occasionally.

Major problems of the world economy

Here I identify what I regard as the principal problems in the world economy and ask whether they can be attributed to the operation of the international monetary system.

Somewhere near the top of the list is the abject poverty of too large a proportion of the world's population. This is an age-old problem. International monetary arrangements can hardly be blamed for its existence.

A related problem is the plight of debt-ridden, middle-income developing countries. Having enjoyed rapid growth in the decades before 1980, they have since then suffered a decline in per capita real income. There is more than one reason for this problem, including insufficient capital inflow from abroad, but it cannot be attributed to the workings of the international monetary system.

The need for economic reform in the Soviet Union and the Eastern European countries has recently come to the fore. These countries must undergo structural and behavioural changes, pollution abatement, new plant and equipment investment, the creation of institutions needed by a market-oriented economy and, no doubt, infusions of capital from abroad. But here, again, nothing in existing international monetary arrangements in the rest of the world has much of a bearing on the existence, or the solution, of the problems facing these countries.

Although Western Europe has enjoyed an economic boom in the past two years, unemployment remains too high there. It averaged 9.6 per cent in the European Community in 1989, compared with a high of 11.3 per cent in 1985. This problem does not appear to have an international monetary cause or solution.

Some observers would include in this list the large payments imbalances on current account among the industrial countries. As noted earlier, it is not evident that these imbalances create an international problem. Clearly, the United States would be better off, now and in the future, if it had not inflicted on itself large budget and current account deficits; or, to put the point differently, if it had maintained its national savings rate at the level of earlier decades. However one regards this problem, the question is, can it be blamed on international monetary arrangements? As was indicated earlier, during most of the 1980s the American current account deficit was financed by private capital flows, as investors abroad were attracted by relatively high United States interest rates, by opportunities for promising direct investments and, possibly, in some periods, by stable political conditions in the face of political uncertainties elsewhere. It is difficult to imagine that different international monetary arrangements would have discouraged such private financing of the oversized United States current account deficits.

Thus, we are left with the two possible reforms referred to above.

International economic policy coordination

The seven largest industrial countries, comprising the Group of Seven—Canada, France, Germany, Italy, Japan, the United Kingdom and the United States—have established a procedure for the coordination of their macroeconomic policies and a related procedure for surveillance of, and some influence over, their exchange rates. We focus here on the macroeconomic coordination process which was authorized at the annual economic summit meetings of the heads of government of the seven countries in 1965 and 1986.

The consultations are carried out at the level of ministers of finance and central bank governors, in the presence of the Managing Director of the IMF, and at the level of finance-ministry deputies, in the presence of the IMF Economic Counsellor. The general purpose of the exercise is to try to assure that the fiscal and monetary policies of the seven countries are compatible with each other and conducive to steady non-inflationary growth of their economies and the world economy. To implement this aim, the deputies, at their frequent unpublicized meetings, with analytical input from the IMF, examine projections of a number of "indicators" of economic performance and policies—both targets and instruments—and draw conclusions as to the desirable direction of policies.

The general rationale underlying this process is that the increase in economic and financial interdependence has had the effect of weakening the domestic impact and strengthening the external impact of policy decisions and non-policy events. If countries' economies have a greater effect on one other, it makes sense to cooperate in the formation of policies. Another way to make this point is to observe that increased interdependence leads to diffusion across borders of the effects of their policy actions; policy coordination is a way to widen the domain of policy-making in recognition of the wider diffusion of policy impacts.

It should be emphasized that what is involved in such a process is in no sense altruism. Nations are not expected to alter their policies for the benefit of others; that would be an unrealistic expectation. Rather, cooperative policy-making brings shared gains or prevents shared losses.

One can point to historical episodes when policy coordination would have produced such gains—for example, in 1972–1973, when all of the industrial countries experienced a burst of inflation, before the large oil-price increase of late 1973, because they all adopted expansionary policies more or less simultaneously and did not take account of the effects on each other and on world commodity prices of that combined expansion of demand. In 1981–1982, after the second oil shock, most industrial countries adopted restrictive monetary, and in some cases fiscal, policies in order to combat severe inflation. Again, they failed to take account of the depressive effects of the policies of other countries and the decline in exports to one another. As a result, the recession of 1981–1982 was deep.

While the potential gains from policy coordination are clear, there are obstacles to its effectiveness. A major obstacle is that, at present, the United States, and perhaps some other countries, have only one policy instrument. Fiscal policy is hobbled in the United States principally by its large budget deficit. But that will not last forever.

Another potential obstacle is that the officials of different nations may operate with different analytical frameworks, that is, differing views on how the world works. If there is disagreement on how policy instruments affect policy targets, agreements on coordinated policies are unlikely. It can be argued that frequent meetings of the officials could resolve this obstacle.

In any event, the coordination process is still in an early stage. It needs a lot of development.

Whether the process can be placed more centrally in the IMF is a valid question. Countries that are not members of the Group of Seven may object to the coordination process as it exists today. Yet, that process, if it is to be effective, requires that officials discuss with each other their policy intentions. Discussion of future policies is a sensitive matter that demands a high degree of confidentiality. Therefore, it must be carried out in a small group. The whole world stands to gain if the Group of Seven nations, which account for more than two thirds of global GNP, succeed in maintaining steady non-inflationary growth. Even so, the resentment of non-participants would be understandable. Such resentment could be alleviated if a way were found for non-members to have an input to the process, perhaps through the Managing Director and the Economic Counsellor of the IMF.

The management of exchange rates

The Bretton Woods par value system was abandoned because it was too rigidly adhered to. The greater mobility of capital put strains on the system, yet Governments were unwilling to adjust par values sufficiently and promptly. But, as noted earlier, those exchange rates that are floating under existing arrangements tend at times to swing too widely.

It seems to follow that present world conditions require greater flexibility of exchange rates than occurred under Bretton Woods but that more management of exchange rates is desirable.

Some degree of exchange rate flexibility is needed for two reasons: (a) even with the increase of trade interdependence, the residents of each country spend much more of their income on home-produced goods and services than on imports, and (b) prices and wages are sticky. The first reason tells us that changes in domestic macroeconomic policies are not sufficient (they may be necessary) to reduce current account imbalances without creating intolerable recessions or inflations; exchange rate changes are also needed. The second reason makes it clear that the principal way to change the price level of one country in relation to another is via changes in exchange rates.

Yet, the large movements of exchange rates in the 1980s, including, at times, speculative bubbles, have had remarkably small effects on trade. For a number of reasons, exporters and importers have become somewhat desensitized to exchange rate changes. The implication of this line of analysis is that there is a case for confining exchange rate movements to narrower ranges—but not necessarily in the immediate future, as St. Augustine might have put it.

The case for delaying reform is that managing exchange rates effectively requires more than coordinated intervention in foreign exchange markets by central banks. It probably also requires that monetary policy be brought into use to influence market rates. But if monetary policy is diverted to this purpose, it will not always be able to perform its main function of assuring non-inflationary growth of economies. One policy instrument cannot be relied on to achieve two targets.

To deal with this problem, it would be necessary to use fiscal policy as the principal instrument for maintaining economies on their non-inflationary growth paths when monetary policy is being aimed at the exchange rate objective.

We may conclude that fiscal policy reform should precede reform of the exchange rate regime.

Chapter 7

THE INTERNATIONAL MONETARY SYSTEM: MURKY WATERS AHEAD

Dragoslav Avramovic*

In chapter 1, Üner Kirdar has drawn attention to the change in the monetary system, which has separated most of the rich from most of the poor countries:

> "In the aftermath of the Second World War, the International Monetary Fund was designed primarily to foster global macroeconomic conditions conducive to the growth of all nations; help countries to promote exchange stability; maintain orderly exchange arrangements; avoid competitive exchange depreciation; monitor world economic trends and international macroeconomic policies; facilitate the expansion and balanced growth of international trade, and contribute thereby to the promotion and maintenance of high levels of employment, real income and the development of the productive resources of all countries.
>
> "None the less, over the past two decades, the major industrialized countries have succeeded in escaping from IMF policy-monitoring. Instead of using their IMF drawing rights, they have chosen to utilize capital market resources, thus avoiding IMF policy prescriptions and adjustment conditionalities. In the 1980s, the Fund's credits, advice and policy subscriptions were limited to developing countries. Major

*Director of Economic Studies, European Centre for Peace and Development, Belgrade; former Director of the Secretariat, Brandt Commission.

– 95 –

industrial powers have chosen to regulate their financial matters according to their own national policy decisions and, whenever required, through consultations restricted to themselves."

Dr. F. Vibert, of the World Institute for Development Economics Research (WIDER), has also commented on this change:

"The international system for supplying liquidity has evolved as a split system, with a sharp and abrupt difference between those countries with access to markets to meet reserve needs and those without access. [The latter] must earn their reserves through exports or through attracting foreign capital, both private and official. Using net foreign receipts gained in this way for reserve purposes involves a high opportunity cost. For those that have lost market access through overindebtedness, the opportunity cost is approximated by the discounts available in the secondary market for their foreign debt. For countries in Central and Eastern Europe now entering fully into global trade and payments arrangements, the costs are also high in comparison with alternative uses of foreign exchange. By contrast, for countries with access to markets, the opportunity cost of reserves simply represents the difference between borrowing costs and the return on holdings."

In this context, we will discuss five issues: the effects on the developed countries and on the international financial situation which they dominate of their ample supply of liquidity; the extent and the effects on the developing countries of the liquidity shortage which most of them are experiencing; the inequality of the international distribution of the burden of adjustment; a possible emergence of regional monetary areas; and the neglected basic objective of international monetary cooperation—full employment.

Effects of quasi-automatic international credit among rich countries

The enormous expansion of United States budgetary deficits and of corporate indebtedness and personal borrowing in almost all rich countries has resulted in outstanding debts and asset prices with few precedents in financial history. United States public and corporate debt tripled in the 1980s. In Japan, the main creditor on international account, the average price-earnings ratio of shares was in excess of 60:1 at the end of 1989, compared to the average of industrialized countries of about 15:1; and real land prices in six major Japanese cities rose 3.5 times in seven years to 1988, reaching fantastic levels. Ratios of gross debt to total assets (book values) of non-financial corporations were 0.81 in Japan and 0.62 in the Federal Republic of Germany in 1986, compared to 0.50 in the United States. Property lending in six countries other than Japan as a percentage of all bank loans to the private sector averaged 27 per cent in 1982 and shot up to 35 per cent in 1989, as real estate speculation accelerated. Quality deterioration occurred, as credit volumes and asset prices continued to increase. In the United States, the credit quality of companies declined at a record pace in the first half of 1990 (for every upgrading of a company debt, there were 4.2 downgrades; in comparison, in 1989 the ratio was 2.5:1 and in the 1982 recession, 2.8:1, all in Moody's Investors Service). Share prices in Japan fell 28 per cent on average in the first quarter of 1990; and even though they recovered more than a third of the loss in the following four months, the future is uncertain, particularly in view of rising interest rates and therefore of rising opportunity costs of holding shares. Property markets have weakened in many places, partly because of excessive construction and partly because of rising interest rates.

Much of the credit and asset price boom would have occurred without a permissive international monetary policy; but this policy, consisting of a continued readiness to hold the currencies of reserve countries and to expand domestic credit on this basis, created an enabling environment for excessive expansion until creditworthiness limits of individual borrowers were reached. But these limits themselves were flexible: as asset prices (shares and real estate) rose, so did the creditworthiness of borrowers. The debt pyramid increases until the debtors are unable to find further creditors willing to finance the debt service on outstanding debt.

The rising level of debt, the corresponding growth of debt-servicing liabilities, the need to finance them and the associated rise in the volume of debt securities have led to pressure on their prices and their obverse, the increase in the rate of interest. Increased risks from exchange rate fluctuations and the fear of, and policy of defence against, inflation have also been at work. Following the major upward shift in the United States rate of interest in the early 1980s and subsequent uneasy stabilization, international interest rates are on the upward march again, this time under the influence of increases in the formerly low-rate financial centres in Germany, Japan and Switzerland. The Swiss and German rates are now at the same level as the United States— 8.5 per cent for a one-year certificate of deposit in the summer of 1990, a development in Switzerland and Germany which would have been considered unbelievable only two years ago. In real terms, international interest rates are two to three times the historical average. It is a major surprise that prices of shares and related securities have stayed so high for so long.

Insufficient supply of international liquidity for developing countries

The present and prospective supply of international liquidity (reserve assets) at the disposal of developing countries is unsatisfactory in relation to demand for three reasons.

First, the volume of gold holdings of developing countries remained stationary during the 1980s, and as the price of gold drifted downwards, the value of these holdings declined by some SDR 10 billion between the end of 1983 and 31 March 1989. There are no prospects that developing countries as a group will increase their gold holdings in view of the pressures on their balances of payment: all additional production, which may be sizeable, is likely to be sold and the proceeds spent on imports or transfers of debt service abroad.

Secondly, the foreign exchange holdings of developing countries increased by some SDR 50 billion between the end of 1983 and 31 March 1989. For developing countries with debt-servicing problems, however, the holdings declined marginally. For most developing countries, no prospects exist for increasing reserves from foreign borrowing on the capital market. This was a major source of supply of reserves during the wave of major borrowing from banks by those countries in the 1970s. With the breakdown of private capital flows to developing countries in 1982, this source of reserve increase has dried out; and while commercial bank lending for trade and specific project finance may revive over time, this will not happen with respect to lending for general balance-of-payments support, including reserve accumulation. Most developing countries will have to earn foreign exchange to augment their reserves, that is, to generate an export surplus which normally will be at the expense of domestic investment or consumption.

Thirdly, the demand of developing countries for external reserve assets is twofold. There will be, first, a regular increase of a "secular" nature in keeping with the growth of the economy and the associated need for an increase in working capital, including cash balances. As the external sector will grow *pari passu* with the rest of the economy over the long run, although not necessarily at the same rate, there will be a corresponding need for adding to external cash (reserve) assets, so that they can keep a customary relationship to rising imports and thus assure their steady flow as needed by the economy as a whole. Then, secondly, an additional increase in demand for reserves occurs in response to fluctuations in payments obligations abroad, which may arise from an export decline, a sudden increase in import demand or an increase in debt payments abroad for external reasons. An example of the latter was an increase of 3 percentage points in the international rate of interest on dollar-denominated loans during 1988. Horst Schulmann, Managing Director of the Institute of International Finance, noted in March 1989 that: "Based on a rule of thumb that every 1 percentage point rise in interest rates adds $4 billion to the debt-servicing costs of the heavily indebted middle-income countries, this would imply an increase of more than $12 billion in the annual interest bill." In addition, there are fluctuations in exports, which have not shown any indications of reduced amplitude in recent years. Gerald K. Helleiner, in a special report on world economic problems, issued in April 1988 by the Institute for International Economics, stated that: "Short-term instability of real and nominal commodity prices and national-level earnings from commodity exports have been sharply higher in recent years than in earlier periods." Alfred Maizels, in discussing the terms of trade and the external financing problems of commodity-exporting developing countries, considered that increased uncertainties concerning the movement of exchange rates, interest rates and the availability of loans on appropriate terms are factors contributing to instability, and he noted a great expansion of speculative activity over the past decade, with funds being transferred into, and out of, a number of important commodity markets, particularly the coffee, sugar and cocoa futures markets among agricultural commodities, and certain non-ferrous metals, particularly copper and tin.

It follows that the present situation penalizes developing countries in two ways. First, as most of them are primary-commodity exporters whose export prices fluctuate widely, their external earnings fluctuate more than the earnings of developed countries; hence, developing countries need proportionately larger reserves to ensure a reasonable stability of their imports and incomes. Secondly, most of them cannot borrow reserves in the capital market and, therefore, have to earn them. Developed countries, which are considered creditworthy, can borrow them; furthermore, those that are reserve currency countries, and, to some extent, even others, can use instruments denominated in their own national currency for payments abroad and hence can dispense to a considerable degree with the need to accumulate external reserve assets.

Issues of SDRs were expected to meet, at least in part, the need for additional reserves: at the time of their creation in 1968, it was expected that the SDR would become a principal unit of account for international transactions, the main medium for reserve transactions and the key means for regulating and supplying global liquidity. In the event, SDRs now account for only 2.4 per cent of total reserves. There have been no SDR allocations in the last four years, thus extending the halt instituted in 1981. The vast majority of countries, both developing and developed, have been in favour of allocations. Opposition has come from three major powers on the grounds that there was plenty of international liquidity around and hence the case for SDR allocations did not exist. What appears to have been forgotten was, first, that fear of inflation, quoted against SDR allocations, did not prevent the leading central banks from creating an enormous amount of international liquidity during the 1980s in supporting their exchange rates; and secondly, that the present distribution of international liquidity between developed and developing countries and between the private and public sectors is so uneven as to threaten both instability and deflation.

No solution to the liquidity problem of a large number of developing countries is in sight at present. The situation is not made easier by the accumulation of arrears by debtor countries to creditors. The total amount of arrears of developing countries to all creditors amounted to $52 billion in December 1988, up from $41 billion at the end of 1987. At the end of 1988, 49 countries were in arrears to their external creditors. For these countries, the future supply of borrowed liquidity is in most cases tied to the solution of the debt problem, and progress here is slow.

Unequal distribution of the adjustment burden

In the negotiations of the Bretton Woods agreements, a major point of discussion concerned the responsibilities of the deficit and the surplus countries, respectively, in the process of adjustment, that is, for closing the financing gap. A fundamental point of theory was that in all cases there were two parties in a financial mishap—the borrower and the lender—and that co-responsibility followed, at least in some degree. The experience with borrowing and lending in the 1920s and with managing the financial aftermath during the Great Depression of the 1930s tended to confirm the theory. What emerged from the Bretton Woods negotiations was the "scarce currency clause"—the right of debtors to apply restrictions on imports from surplus countries.

Practice in the last 20 years, and particularly in the 1980s, has moved in the opposite direction: it was the debtors that were asked by the creditors/lenders to liberalize their imports, in the belief that import competition would compel the domestic producers to improve efficiency and thus enable the debtor's economy as a whole to become a competitive exporter. There is truth in this argument to a degree. But in practice it frequently means that the imports of the developing country need to rise when it already has a deficit, when it has a limited or non-existent capital inflow and when the only way it can meet the additional import demand is by devaluing even more than would be necessary otherwise. This devaluation will normally lead to a deterioration in the terms of trade, and it will also exacerbate domestic inflation.

No corresponding pressure on creditor countries to liberalize their imports exists, as most developing country debtors either do not have sufficient leverage or have not been able to exert it. The only international deficit country which has managed to turn the tables has been the United States: it is the United States which has exerted continuing pressure on the main creditors to change their trade and other policies so as to accommodate additional imports (or curtail exports) and thus help the United States balance of payments. But the case of the United states as a debtor is unique, in import purchasing power, production and technological capacity, and military weight. More generally, most developing country debtors have been at a disadvantage, and this has adversely affected both their terms of trade and terms of capital inflow.

Emergence of regional monetary areas

The idea that the world is moving towards regional monetary blocs has been current for some time. British Prime Minister Thatcher gave it political prominence at the Houston meeting of the Group of Seven major industrialized countries in July 1990, when she stated that "there are three regional groups at this summit, one based on the dollar, one based on the yen, one on the deutsche mark", and warned that "industrial powers may fall into three inward-looking blocs: the United States, Canada and parts of Latin America; Europe, with the European

Community at its centre; and the Pacific nations, led by Japan but including its regional trading partners".

Growing diversification of foreign exchange reserves away from the United States dollar has given impetus to thinking on the subject of regional monetary areas. In the mid-1970s, reserves held in United States dollars accounted for almost 80 per cent of the total reserves. This proportion is now down to 61 per cent. The deutsche mark now accounts for 21 per cent of total foreign exchange reserves and the yen for 8 per cent, both almost double the shares they held in the early 1980s. Paradoxically, movement away from the United States dollar appears to have accelerated in 1989, even though it was strengthening then; furthermore, United States foreign reserves other than gold, at $66 billion in May 1990, were one third higher than a year earlier and second only to Japan's $73.8 billion. (Taking both gold at market prices and foreign exchange holdings, United States total reserves still greatly exceed those of Japan and Germany: $161.6 billion for the United States, compared to $82.4 billion for Japan and $96.5 billion for Germany, in March 1990. United States gold holdings at 262 million ounces represent 28 per cent of the world total, compared to 2.6 per cent for Japan and 10.1 per cent for Germany.)

Regional monetary areas would mean that the exchange rates of smaller countries within a region would be tied to the currency of the regional centre, while the mutual exchange rates between the centres may float or be fixed. There is no evidence that the potential three regional centres are now thinking of fixing the mutual rates any closer than in the present vague "target zones" which perhaps exist. The main efforts are currently focused on intraregional relations (European Community), within-country fiscal and corporate finance problems (United States), and worldwide trade relations and disputes (Japan, the United States, the European Community, developing countries and others).

The idea of basing the international monetary system on agreed fixed relations among key currencies and letting the rest of the currencies be organized around these—the "key currency approach"—was discussed during and after the Bretton Woods negotiations. John H. Williams, Vice-President of the New York Federal Reserve, was the main proponent of this idea. He also foresaw the possibility that the IMF would end up being of relevance only to "exchange-poor" countries.

Regional centres may be important for developing countries as possible sources of emergency assistance in balance-of-payments crises. The IMF was established to act momentarily in periods of balance-of-payments stress in order to prevent such stress from having adverse effects on trade, employment and welfare, because the experience of the 1930s had show that ad hoc deals among central banks to provide support were difficult to organize in a hurry. We are back at ad hoc deals, however, as it takes a long time—months and sometimes even more than a year—to negotiate agreements between the countries and the IMF, and in the meantime bridging assistance needs to be negotiated with central banks or private banks, or both. The present situation is that of needing a bridge to a bridge; otherwise, crisis and deflation may spread, with a reduction in imports, employment and welfare— that is, the very things the Bretton Woods agreements were intended to prevent. Practice has suggested that regional centres—for example, the United States Federal Reserve *vis-à-vis* Latin American countries and some others, and emerging activities in Western Europe *vis-à-vis* Eastern Europe—may provide bridging assistance quickly. What is involved here is a complementary relationship between the worldwide and the regional financial centres rather than one of substitution.

Full employment: the neglected objective

Michel Beaud, in an article in *Le Monde* on 22 May 1990, referred to Keynes, the co-founder of international financial institutions:

> "'Two fundamental flaws of the economic world in which we live are, first, that full employment is not assured, and secondly, that distribution of wealth and income is arbitrary and lacks equity,' wrote J. M. Keynes in the concluding notes of the *General Theory* in 1935. These propositions, regretfully, hold equally true in 1990. The essence of the problem is that, since the return of massive unemploy-

ment, we have not known how to define a full-employment policy adapted to present circumstances. Do we need, once again, a wave of racism and nationalism; do we need the attachment of desperate masses to totalitarian ideologies; do we need new wars for the men in power to engage themselves, as they did in the years 1950 and 1960, in a struggle against these 'fundamental flaws' which today are growing again and spreading across the world?"

Dr. Forte, an important Italian political figure, calls full employment the central issue of international efforts in the immediate future:

"While the case for full employment was in the forefront of the efforts to promote a new economic order after the Second World War, this objective seems downgraded today. It would be paradoxical that while the perspective of a new great war is increasingly vanishing, the full use of our resources and good will to promote full employment was not considered the most desirable perspective of this peaceful system of international relations."

The room for improvement is large. Some reform programmes imply massive unemployment. Some writers and officials argue that the more ruthless a policy in throwing people out of work the greater the compliments and rewards it should get. There is no specific plan on how to reverse unemployment, no estimate of how long it may take or of what will happen to real wages in the meantime. Economics and public policy should be able to do better.

Chapter 8

COORDINATING MACROECONOMIC POLICIES

Peter B. Kenen*

Several economists have criticized Governments for trying to coordinate their national policies. The obstacles are large, they say, the potential gains are small, and Governments may get it wrong, making matters worse. Some of them were skeptical before coordination started to become popular with Governments. In 1981, for example, Max Corden argued that coordination is not necessary because the international monetary "non-system" has its own logic:

> "The key feature of the present system is that it is a form of international laissez-faire. First of all, it allows free play to the private market, not just to trade in goods and non-financial services but, above all, to the private capital market. Secondly, it allows free play to Governments and their central banks to operate in the market and—if they wish and where they can—to influence and even fix its prices or its quantities. Thus, it is a fairly free market where many Governments, acting in their own presumed interests and not necessarily taking much account of the interests of other Governments, are participants."[1]

In Corden's "market" view of the monetary system, each Government can and should be free to choose its own monetary and fiscal

---

*Walker Professor of Economics and International Finance and Director of the International Finance Section, Princeton University. This paper draws on one presented at the October 1988 Conference on International Policy Coordination and Exchange Rate Fluctuations, sponsored by the National Bureau of Economic Research.

policies, and it should also choose its exchange rate arrangements and decide whether to borrow or lend on international capital markets. This sort of decentralization might well be optimal if all economies were very small; each country's decisions regarding its exchange rate would have only trivial effects on other countries' effective exchange rates and its decisions about borrowing and lending would not have much influence on world interest rates.

What happens, however, when economies are large? Each country's policies affect other countries, and structural interdependence gives rise, in turn, to policy interdependence. The conventional case for coordination starts here. But the strength of the case depends on the extent and character of the underlying structural interdependence, the Governments' own objectives and the number of policy instruments they have at their command.

The critics of coordination are castigating Governments for pursuing objectives that bear very little resemblance to the objectives that actually animate the Governments' own efforts.

Most economists adopt a policy-optimizing approach to coordination, and because they use game-theoretic methods to represent it, they tend to treat the participating Governments as antagonists engaged in policy barter—the trading of commitments about policy instruments without any trading of analyses or forecasts. In this framework, moreover, exchange rate stabilization does not play a major role; it is one method for optimizing policies but a second-best method at that.

Governments, by contrast, appear to adopt a regime-preserving or public-goods approach to coordination. It has different implications for the ways in which Governments interact and for the role of exchange rate stabilization. Mutual persuasion takes the place of adversarial bargaining, and exchange rate stabilization becomes a public good rather than a rule for optimizing policies. Furthermore, the regime-preserving approach sheds light on certain puzzling questions. Why does policy coordination move in and out of fashion? Why are disagreements about policy objectives cited so often as "obstacles" to coordination, when in fact standard policy-optimizing models show that they should raise the gains from coordination? Why do Governments argue about sharing the "burdens" of coordination, when each of them should be expected to gain from policy optimization?

Perspectives on policy coordination

Governments cooperate in many ways. They trade information about their economies, policies and forecasts. They provide financial assistance to other Governments, bilaterally and multilaterally, ranging from balance-of-payments support to long-term development aid. They act jointly to supervise or regulate various sorts of economic activity.

Coordination is the most rigorous type of international cooperation because it involves mutually agreed modifications in national policies. In the macroeconomic domain, it involves an exchange of explicit, operational commitments about the conduct of monetary and fiscal policies. Commitments often can be framed contingently, with reference to mutually agreed norms or targets; a Government can promise to cut taxes, for example, if the growth rate of real or nominal GNP is lower than the rate it has promised to deliver. But commitments to targets, by themselves, do not constitute coordination. Commitments about instruments are the distinguishing feature of coordination, setting it apart from other forms of economic cooperation.

Forms of coordination

Coordination can result from episodic bargains about specific policy packages or from a once-for-all bargain to follow some set of policy rules.

The Bonn summit in 1978 is usually cited as the leading instance of an episodic bargain, although it was not confined to macroeconomic matters. Germany and Japan made promises about their fiscal policies, and the United states made promises about its energy policies. The Bretton Woods Agreement of 1944 is frequently cited as a once-for-all bargain about rules, although it was too vague to meet the definition of full-fledged coordination. The exchange rate obligations were explicit; the corresponding policy commitments were implicit, but the latter became somewhat tighter as the Bretton Woods system evolved. The

International Monetary Fund began to attach strict conditions to the use of its resources, and Working Party 3 of the Organisation for Economic Cooperation and Development devoted close attention to the macroeconomic side of the exchange rate system. The duties of deficit countries were more clearly defined and commonly accepted than those of surplus countries. Nevertheless, the obligations were mutual in an important contingent sense. They applied in principle to every country when it ran a balance-of-payments deficit.

The Louvre Accord, reached in Paris in February 1987, can be described as a combination of the two techniques for policy coordination. It included rule-based obligations, too loosely defined perhaps, linking the use of interest rate policies to the maintenance of stable exchange rates. It included an ad hoc bargain about fiscal policies, although it served mainly to codify goals that Governments had already chosen unilaterally.

A number of rule-based systems have been proposed in recent years, including those of McKinnon (1984, 1988),[2] Meade (1984)[3] and Williamson and Miller (1987).[4] McKinnon advocates a gold standard without gold. The major central banks would choose an appropriate rate for global monetary growth and would then conduct their monetary policies to realize that rate. Furthermore, they would peg exchange rates by non-sterilized intervention, which would make a country's money supply grow more rapidly than the global rate when its currency was strong, and grow less rapidly than the global rate when its currency was weak. The system would work symmetrically, however, so that exchange rate pegging would not affect the global rate. Williamson and Miller would not peg exchange rates, but their plan is more comprehensive. It would cover fiscal policies as well as interest rate or monetary policies.

The policy-optimizing approach

Many economists look upon policy formation as an optimizing process and are thus inclined to view coordination as an extension of that process. Each Government is deemed to maximize a welfare function defined in terms of its policy targets; in the formulation used by most of the studies cited below, it sets its policy instruments, interest rates, tax rates and so on to minimize some weighted sum of differences between ideal and actual values of its target variables, such as the growth rate of real GNP and the inflation rate.

When economies are interdependent, one Government's decisions are likely to affect other Governments' decisions, but it is deemed to disregard that possibility. If all of them act this way, however, they will wind up in a suboptimal situation, known as the non-cooperative or Nash equilibrium. They can reach a better outcome, known as the cooperative or Pareto equilibrium, by changing the settings of their policy instruments in a mutually agreed manner. Each Government can get closer to its policy targets and thus raise the value of its welfare function. The increase in the value of the welfare function is, of course, the measure of the gain from policy coordination.

Viewed from this standpoint, policy coordination can be seen as a way of internalizing the effects of economic interdependence, which no single Government can do by setting its policies unilaterally. Policy coordination gives each Government partial control over other Governments' policy instruments. Therefore, it relieves the shortage of instruments that keeps each Government from reaching its own targets.

No one can quarrel with the logic of the policy-optimizing approach. It has given precise operational meaning to policy interdependence, provided a framework for measuring the costs of neglecting it and linked this special subject with the much larger literature on macroeconomic theory and policy. But this approach is more normative than positive. It tells us what could be achieved by multinational optimization under ideal conditions and warns against some of the risks. It is less useful, however, in helping us to understand what Governments actually want to accomplish, the obstacles they face and the institutional arrangements they employ. In this sense, the policy-optimizing approach resembles the traditional theory of international trade, which shows that free trade is the best of all possible policies from a cosmopolitan perspective but neglects the effects of rigidities and imperfections in the economy and does not address the processes that shape trade policies.

The regime-preserving approach

Some economists, many political scientists and most policy makers look at policy coordination from a different standpoint. It is needed to produce certain public goods and defend the international economic system from economic and political shocks, including misbehaviour by Governments themselves.

This important work was done by the United States in the early post-war decades. The United States was the hegemonic power, with the capacity and self-interested concern to stabilize the world economy unilaterally. Furthermore, it had been chiefly responsible for writing the rules of the Bretton Woods system and designing the institutions. It could thus be expected to defend them whenever they were threatened. Equally important, other Governments could not accomplish very much without American cooperation.

Matters are quite different now. It is still hard to get very far without American cooperation, and little is likely to happen until Washington decides that something must be done. But the United States cannot act alone. The costs are too high.

It is easy to find examples of regime-preserving cooperation in recent economic history. They include the mobilization of financial support for the dollar and sterling in the 1960s and the joint management of the London gold pool, the "rescue" of the dollar in 1978, the speedy provision of bridge loans to Mexico at the start of the debt crisis in 1982, and the Plaza communiqué issued in New York in September 1985, which was meant to defend the trade regime rather than alter the exchange rate regime. The bargain struck at Bonn in 1978 can likewise be described as regime-preserving coordination. It reflected an agreed need to act on two fronts: for more vigorous recovery from the global recession of 1974–75 to combat rising unemployment, especially in

Europe; and for energy conservation to reduce the industrial countries' dependence on imported oil and limit the ability of the Organization of Petroleum Exporting Countries to raise oil prices.

When viewed from this different perspective, policy coordination becomes the logical response to the dispersion of power and influence that ended United States hegemony. Public goods must be produced and institutional arrangements defended by common or collective action. When seen this way, moreover, disagreements about the benefits and costs of policy coordination take on a different but familiar aspect. They become debates about burden-sharing.

Finally, the regime-preserving view gives us a different way to look at exchange rate management. Seen from the policy-optimizing viewpoint, it represents the use of a simple policy rule to internalize or limit the effect of economic interdependence. The results are frequently inferior to those of full-fledged optimization, but reliance on a simple rule minimizes the need for ad hoc bargaining, diminishes the danger of cheating or reneging and shortens the lags involved in dealing with new situations. Seen from the regime-preserving viewpoint, by contrast, collective exchange rate management represents an attempt to improve the global economic environment by pursuing exchange rate stability as a policy objective or, more precisely, as an intermediate objective conducive to the pursuit of stable and liberal trade policies and an efficient allocation of resources, nationally and globally.

Obstacles to policy coordination

Some economists have used the policy-optimizing framework to measure the potential gains from policy coordination and have found that the gains were disappointingly small. For instance, the coordination of fiscal and monetary policies by Germany, Japan and the United States had very little influence on the fiscal instruments and rather small effects on economic performance; when measured in units equivalent to percentage-point changes in real income, the welfare gains were smaller than 1 per cent of GNP.

Why is it that Governments do not exploit those gains? Four reasons are commonly given. First, Governments are apt to renege on their bargains and thus distrust each other; secondly, Governments hold different views about economic behaviour and the workings of the world economy; thirdly, Governments have different policy targets; and fourthly, political and constitutional constraints interfere with the bargaining process.

The first explanation has been demolished. The rest make sense, but some of them seem more cogent when they are invoked to explain the apparent scarcity of regime-preserving coordination rather than the failure to exploit opportunities for policy-optimizing coordination.

Reneging and reliability

The concern about reneging derives in large part from the stylized way in which economists have represented public and private decision-making and the resulting concern with the problem of time consistency. Wages and prices are set by the private sector in the light of its expectations concerning the inflation rate, which depends in turn on its expectations concerning the money supply. If the Government promises to raise the money supply by, say, 5 per cent and the private sector expects the Government to keep its word, wages and prices will rise immediately by 5 per cent, in line with the expected growth rate of the money supply. At this point, the Government has two options. If it keeps its promise, it will exactly validate the actual inflation rate and there will be no change in output or employment. If it breaks its promise and raises the money supply faster, it can stimulate output and employment, because the inflation rate cannot change until wages and prices can be adjusted. If the Government breaks its word frequently, however, it will lose credibility. The private sector will begin to disregard the Government's promises and start to base its expectations on the actual growth rate of the money supply. The inflation rate will rise, and the more rapid growth rate of the money supply will serve merely to validate the higher inflation rate. It will cease to stimulate output and employment.

The argument, however, depends on three assumptions: (1) the private sector makes binding decisions about wages and prices; (2) the Government can and should make promises about its own behaviour to facilitate planning by the private sector; and (3) the "game" played by the Government *vis-à-vis* the private sector is the only game in town.

The assumption about binding private-sector decisions is unexceptional. In fact, the resulting stickiness of wages and prices is the fundamental reason for wanting to stabilize nominal exchange rates. When wages and prices are sticky, changes in nominal exchange rates lead to changes in real exchange rates, which affect the level, location and composition of economic activity. The case for predictable behaviour by Governments is equally hard to challenge in principle but has to be qualified carefully. Predictability can reduce economic instability, but Governments may need to keep markets guessing by creating uncertainty about their own tactics, and a dogged dedication to predictability can increase instability in an uncertain world.

Governments play many games simultaneously, including the all-important political game. If a government cheats on any other player, all of them can punish it. In fact, they can replace it at the next election. The costs of cheating, moreover, are very high in the international domain. Governments that break their promises to other Governments cannot make more bargains with them. This consideration is particularly important for the major industrial countries, which have to cooperate not only on macroeconomic matters but on many economic, political and strategic issues.

Governments try to refrain from making commitments they cannot expect to honour and try to honour those they make.

Disagreements about economic behaviour

Governments do disagree about economic behaviour. The American and German Governments have disagreed for years about the responsiveness of unemployment to aggregate demand and even about the way that aggregate demand responds to fiscal and monetary policies.

For a time, moreover, United States officials denied that there was any connection between the United States budget and trade deficits, and other Governments connected them simplistically, without making room for the role of the exchange rate.

When Governments disagree about the workings of the world economy, they are bound to hold different views about the costs of coordination, even when they agree completely about the benefits. Suppose that two Governments are considering the use of interest-rate policies to stabilize exchange rates. If they hold different views about the way that interest rates affect aggregate demand, they will disagree about the costs of exchange rate stabilization.

Disagreements about economic behaviour may be very potent in preventing this sort of coordination. If Governments are willing to contemplate policy-optimizing coordination, they must believe that a policy bargain will allow them to make welfare-improving changes in their own national policies. When they come to contemplate regime-preserving coordination, they may still believe that their own national policies are optimal and will thus want their partners to make the policy changes required for the common good.

Disagreements about policy objectives

The same possibility arises when Governments have different policy objectives—the third reason for the apparent scarcity of policy coordination. In fact, such differences cannot explain why Governments fail to engage in policy-optimizing coordination. They should make it more attractive. Governments that have incompatible objectives can nevertheless benefit from policy coordination.

Consider two identical economies with rigid wage rates and greedy Governments. Each Government wants to hold three quarters of the global gold stock, so that there is clear conflict between their objectives. If they pursue their targets independently, raising their interest rates competitively to attract capital inflows and gold, they will wind up with identical gold stocks but high unemployment rates. There are two ways to deal with this outcome. The two Governments can agree to reduce their interest rates without even talking about their targets. That is the sort of policy barter that many economists have in mind when they talk about policy-optimizing coordination. Alternatively, the Governments can reveal and modify their targets. But what if they reveal them and refuse to modify them? That is when conflicts or differences in targets obstruct coordination.

This case is too simple to take seriously—or is it? It does not differ fundamentally from the case in which Governments pursue incompatible current account targets, and they seem to do that frequently. It does not differ from the case in which they attach different weights to different targets, including common or collective targets that they can achieve only at some cost in terms of their domestic targets. When common targets are at issue, moreover, debates about objectives are unavoidable. The aims of the exercise have to be identified, and differences in preferences are bound to surface. When Governments engage in policy barter, they can bargain about means without discussing ends. When they engage in mutual persuasions, which is what normally happens, it is hard to agree on means without agreeing on ends.

Political and constitutional constraints

The fourth reason for the shortage of coordination applies to both varieties. Once again, however, it provides a more compelling explanation for the scarcity of regime-preserving coordination. Political and constitutional constraints interfere with every form of international cooperation, but they are hardest to surmount when the costs are clearer and closer to home than the benefits.

The political obstacles to policy coordination have been dramatized by the budgetary problems of the United States. How can the United States engage in international bargaining about fiscal policies when Congressional leaders can say that the President's budget is "dead on arrival" on Capitol Hill? In the last days of the First World War, the German General Staff was said to believe that the situation was serious but not hopeless, while the Austrian General staff thought that it was hopeless but not serious. The Viennese view may be more appropriate here. The budgetary deadlock of the 1980s does not signify permanent paralysis. Nor should we neglect the political problems faced by other major countries in making and adjusting fiscal policies.

Once the German and Japanese Governments have decided to make a policy change, they can commit themselves formally; the United States Government cannot, because it cannot commit the Congress. But the record is not so very bad. President Carter was careful not to promise more than he could deliver, and he did deliver eventually. In another context, moreover, the White House obtained in advance a commitment to rapid Congressional action on the trade-policy bargain produced by the Tokyo round of negotiations of the General Agreement on Tariffs and Trade—the "fast track" that Congress would follow in agreeing to accept or reject those parts of the bargain requiring new legislation. A similar stand-by arrangement might be included in the fiscal-policy package that is used to break the budgetary deadlock.

The basic problems are political, not constitutional. Democratic governments cannot make major policy changes without working hard to persuade the public that the new policies will be better than the old, if not, indeed, the best of all possible policies. In brief, fiscal policies are not very flexible in any democracy, regardless of its constitution.

Policy coordination is made more difficult by jurisdictional divisions within Governments. The problem is most serious on the monetary side, especially in Germany and the United States, which have independent central banks. Here again, however, constitutional arrangements matter less than political realities, and independent central banks maintain their independence by being sensitive to those realities. They cannot permit politicians to pre-commit them or take their consent for granted, and they make their views known, privately or publicly. Once they have given their consent, however, they are very reliable partners, because credibility is their most important asset. Furthermore, they depend on each other to protect their independence. On several occasions, central banks appear to have postponed interest rate changes until they could be sure that foreign central banks would move with them.

Finally, monetary policies can be altered rapidly and incrementally, without building a new political consensus. That is why a change in monetary policy tends to be the first signal of a change in official thinking about the economic outlook. Monetary policies can be coordinated more deftly than fiscal policies, despite jurisdictional divisions in some countries.

The framework for policy coordination

Rigidities in making fiscal policies and analytical disagreements about the ways in which they work may be sufficient to account for the apparent scarcity of policy-optimizing coordination—why Governments fail to exploit all of the potential gains. They may even account for a more important failure. Quantitative studies of policy coordination have to start with a benchmark—the counterpart of the non-cooperative equilibrium. Hence, they must define an optimal set of policies for each Government acting unilaterally, and this is an instructive exercise. The welfare gains obtained by optimizing policies prove to be larger than the gains obtained thereafter by moving from noncooperative to cooperative policies.

The same rigidities and disagreements also help to account for the apparent scarcity of regime-preserving coordination, and disagreements about targets are important, too. They combine to produce disagreements about burden-sharing. But these disagreements are more readily susceptible of resolution than those that arise when one Government tries to tell another how to pursue its own self-interest. For this reason if no other, we can perhaps be optimistic about the prospects for the sorts of policy coordination required to sustain exchange rate management.

What sorts of coordination are needed? Intervention and interest rate differences may be used to stabilize exchange rates, while the global average of real interest rates and national fiscal policies could be used to regulate aggregate demand. Conflicts between external and internal balance could be reconciled in the usual way, by periodic adjustments in real exchange rates.

However, while monetary policies must be coordinated closely to influence capital flows and offset expectations of exchange rate realignments, they cannot be assigned to that task exclusively, nor can fiscal policies be assigned exclusively to managing aggregate demand. On the one hand, fiscal policies affect current account balances and, therefore, the size of the task faced by monetary policies. On the other hand, fiscal policies cannot be adjusted frequently enough to stabilize aggregate demand. Monetary policies must do some of the work that fiscal policies could do if they were more flexible, and exchange rate changes must do the rest.

It is important to distinguish between exchange rate management and the rigid defence of pegged rates within very narrow bands. Bands should be hard but wide and should be adjusted frequently to rectify disequilibria, including those resulting from rigid fiscal policies. It is also important to distinguish between fiscal differences and fiscal shocks. International differences in fiscal policies do not necessarily destabilize exchange rates. They have not done so in the European Monetary System, even though they continue to be quite large. In fact, differences in fiscal policies can compensate for differences in savings rates that tend by themselves to produce current account imbalances. The lessons to be learned from the 1980s relate to the effects of large fiscal shocks, which are bad news indeed, and the framework for multilateral surveillance currently being developed by the Group of Seven Governments should focus sharply on that problem.

Notes

1. W. M. Corden, "The logic of the international monetary non-system", in *Reflections on a Troubled World Economy: Essays in Honour of Herbert Giersch,* edited by F. Machlup, G. Fels and H. Muller-Groeling (London, St. Martins Press, 1981), p. 60.

2. R. I. McKinnon, "An international standard for monetary stabilization", in *Policy Analyses in International Economics, No. 8* (Washington, D.C., Institute for International Economics, 1984), and "Monetary and exchange rate policies for international stability: a proposal", in *Journal of Economic Perspectives,* Winter 1988, pp. 83–103.

3. J. E. Meade, "A new Keynesian Bretton Woods", in *Three Banks Review*, June 1984.

4. J. Williamson and M. H. Miller, "Targets and indicators: a blueprint for the international coordination of economic policies", in *Policy Analyses in International Economics, No. 22* (Washington, D.C., Institute for International Economics, 1987).

Chapter 9

THE INTERNATIONAL MONETARY SYSTEM: MORE COORDINATION OR MORE COMPETITION?

Emre Gönensay*

Discussions of the international monetary system take the core of this system—national monetary systems—as given and then attempt to develop proposals for the improvement of the superstructure, that is, the international system. But there are major problems connected with our existing structure of national monetary systems which should be addressed first. Failure to do this may cause theorizing about the improvement of the international monetary system to be out of focus.

One of the major concerns in this area is maintaining stability of exchange rates. If separate national monetary systems did not consistently produce price instabilities, exchange rate instabilities would not arise as a global problem.

Why do national monetary systems tend perennially to produce price instabilities? And what has been done so far to remedy this tendency?

This paper addresses some of the basic issues which are relevant to this question. These issues are fundamental to a proper evaluation of the international monetary system. They may also lead to questions not easily answerable or may indicate unorthodox approaches. Neverthe-

*Professor of Economics, University of Boğaziçi, Istanbul.

less, they are appropriate at this turning-point in history when so many radical changes are taking place.

National monetary systems: the orthodoxy of government monopoly

The primary objective of a monetary system should be to achieve price stability. Experience shows that monetary change can produce real change only temporarily, if at all. Therefore, the narrowing down of our monetary objectives to price stability is justified. But most of the domestic monetary systems persistently fail to achieve price stability and therefore cause inflation of varying rates most of the time.

Failure to achieve domestic price stability in individual countries becomes, then, one of the major factors causing exchange rate instability and/or balance-of-payments disequilibria. In turn, the attempt to achieve exchange rate stability and balance-of-payments equilibria is the chief concern of international policy coordination. It is as if, having failed at one primary level and taking it for granted, people are searching for a second-best solution.

It seems that much thinking and conceptualizing is still needed at the primary level of domestic monetary systems.

There is, in fact, one unique system in the world today characterizing the monetary systems of different countries: it is the system made up of a single "token" currency the issue of which is monopolized (nationalized) by the single monetary authority and backed by law as legal tender.

Looking back at the history of money, one can accept the invention of commodity money, and thus the move away from barter, as an efficient and logical step. Equally, the creation of token money can be considered a necessary and efficient move. But can we say the same about the unique organization of that "token" paper standard under a nationalized monopoly?

There is much in the history of money to suggest that this unique system was a political outcome, arising out of the wishes of rulers and governments to extend their political power into the economic sphere and, in any case, reap the benefits of seniorage, rather than the outcome of any necessity to consider efficiency.

Although history is rich with examples suggesting the above, the mainstream of monetary theory is somewhat silent on this fundamental question. Regardless of how one views the development of the unique monetary system, if one is dissatisfied with it, and dissatisfied one must be, if one fails persistently to achieve price stability, then consideration of the ways by which it can be improved or changed is in order.

Reforming the system

The underlying theme of all attempts to reform the nationalized monopolistic monetary systems centres around the depoliticization of monetary management. This must arise from a tacit acceptance that the marriage of seniorage and political power leads to a misuse of this power for political ends and hence to price instability and bouts of inflation.

Five main thrusts of reform can be identified in history, all aiming at the depoliticization of currency issue. One is to establish the "autonomy" of central banks by legal charter, rendering them independent from the government and thus shielding them from political influence. A second tack centres around attempts to constitutionalize the balanced-budget principle. This would attack the core of the problem by eliminating the means by which seniorage may be misused. A third line is that taken by advocates of rigid monetary rules. In this case, even the central bank, whether independent or not, would be circumscribed by the pre-set monetary rules. Monetary targeting, prevalent and fashionable now, is a diluted form of this practice. A fourth way is the acceptance of the convertibility principle. This is the anchoring of the national currency at a fixed rate to another "standard" and the undertaking by the monetary authority to defend convertibility at that given rate. Finally, schemes of monetary union may also be seen ultimately as reform efforts in the same vein, since they would very effectively "depoliticize" national monies by doing away with them. The hope, of course, is that the supranational monetary authority which would be created would itself be autonomous and apolitical.

Unfortunately, these many different efforts at reform have not as yet been successful; price instability and inflation are still with us, despite long years of tinkering with various mixtures of the above-mentioned recipes.

One cannot help but reflect that most of the reforms that have been considered leave management of the monetary system basically to the discretion of a single individual or a few individuals. At a time when we seem to be reaching a consensus that economies are best when managed by systems—that is, competition under free markets—and not by individuals, it is surprising that we are content to leave the management of the core of these economies to individuals. Perhaps the real problem lies here.

Alternative monetary systems: competition and the privatization of national monies

A number of economists who have questioned the wisdom of a discretionary monetary system under government monopoly have taken a radically different tack and examined the possibility of a system of private competing currencies. Notable among these are F.A. Hayek, Benjamin Klein and Gordon Tullock.[1]

Hayek's proposal is to privatize money. It is a complex and elaborate system in which many different private banks issue their own different and distinguishable monies and undertake to keep their value stable in terms of a chosen basket of commodities. Competition ensures that each bank has a very strong vested interest in keeping the value of its money stable. Otherwise, unlike a government monopoly, the central bank, it would go out of business—hence, the superiority of the system over nationalized money in producing stable prices.

Some of the problems that may arise within such a system and how the market would deal with them have been discussed at some length by Hayek. Our aim is not to go into a detailed evaluation of the proposal but simply to identify it for future consideration. No matter how radical and impractical it may seem at first sight, the proposal nevertheless addresses some of the fundamental issues related to present-day problems. For example, the notion of parallel competing national currencies, which was always an alternative undercurrent in the discussions of European Monetary Union, is a case in point, because it encompasses part of the Hayek idea—that is, competing currencies within national borders, although these currencies are not private but are issued by different national monopolies.

In fact, while thinking about the Hayek proposal, I came to the unexpected conclusion—unexpected to me at least—that in reforming the monetary system it was perhaps competition which is of crucial importance and not whether money is privatized or not, for if a sufficient number of national monopolies can be made to compete, then effectively they cease to be monopolists. It is with this conceptual framework that I want to look ahead, in the next section, to the future.

The future: a move towards competing national currencies?

We are witnessing today rapid and widespread deregulation of foreign exchange markets and the dismantling of foreign exchange controls in individual countries. This decontrol extends to capital transactions as well, so that more and more national currencies are now becoming convertible, including those of many least developed countries.

It is well known through experience that if a national monetary authority resorts to serious abuse of its currency, widespread currency substitution can take place even under the strictest regime of foreign exchange controls.

Under a regime of free foreign exchange markets and convertibility, this tendency towards currency substitution would be much stronger, easier to achieve and the norm rather than the exception. In fact, many newcomers to convertibility are now experiencing this phenomenon even though their inflation rates are mild by historical standards. In short, we seem to be moving towards a world where national currency markets are no longer protected but are integrated to each other.

This is quite distinct from the often talked about integration of financial markets and would lead to even more fundamental consequences, because a system of parallel competing currencies, about which some theoretical work exists and which is sometimes considered as an alternative to European Monetary Union, is, in fact, gradually establishing itself across the world spontaneously.

In such a world, the monopoly of national central banks would only be nominal because each would effectively face competition of other central bank monies within its own borders. Since it is holders of money that value its stability of purchasing power most, the competitive discipline of such a system would foster price stability.

If these conclusions are correct, then many of the problems with which international monetary reform is now preoccupied will be eliminated with further progress towards the integration of currency markets.

Instead of concentrating their efforts on coordination of central bank policies, should not Governments do the opposite and help in the establishment of a framework of more competition among them?

Finally, if a system of universally competing parallel currencies, in which each currency becomes a perfect substitute for every other currency, is a success, would this not, in fact, be a market solution equivalent to the Utopia of "world monetary union" and a most significant step towards the integration of the world economy?

Notes

1. F.A. Hayek, "Denationalization of money", Hobart Paper, IEA, London, 1978; Benjamin Klein, "The competitive supply of money", in *Journal of Money, Credit and Banking,* November 1975; Gordon Tullock, "Competing moneys", in *Journal of Money, Credit and Banking,* 1976.

Chapter 10

CAPITAL MARKETS: NEW MEANS OF INTERNATIONAL FINANCING

Christine Bogdanowicz-Bindert*

A t present, any effort on the part of banks in the industrialized nations to supply fresh funds to rescheduling countries will have to overcome stiff opposition from shareholders, regulators, depositors and employees. This opposition, when taken within the context of the lingering country debt that remains on the balance sheets of most banks and the stiffer capital guidelines to be imposed internationally by 1992, will effectively take loans from private sector banks out of the financing picture for developing countries into the medium term.

The multilateral financial institutions will, of course, remain in the picture, but here political questions arise on both sides of the table. Can a country afford the luxury of putting all its eggs in one basket—in this case the World Bank/International Monetary Fund? If relationships with multilateral financial institutions grow too strong, will domestic political problems emerge? If these questions do not dominate the thinking of finance ministers, they certainly weigh heavily on the minds of their bosses. From the viewpoint of the industrialized nations, at what point does multilateral support take on foreign aid connotations and enter the political realm, especially when tangible economic

*President of River Partners, Frankfurt am Main, Germany; former Senior Vice-President, International Banking Division, Shearson Lehman, American Express.

progress on the part of the borrowers is slow or nonexistent? These are pertinent questions which dominate today's international financial relations.

If countries that have rescheduled intend to integrate in the world economic community on an arm's-length basis, their only viable approach beyond the politically risky multilaterals is to tap into the capital markets. Therefore, sovereigns, particularly the transitional economies of Central and Eastern Europe, will undoubtedly have to make greater use of the world's capital markets to satisfy their future external financing needs.

This, of course, is easier said than done because the image of the rescheduling countries has also been tarnished in the international capital markets. It should be noted that several Central European countries do not suffer from this handicap but face other challenges, including perceptions of political instability. To make this a doubly difficult issue, the world's capital markets have undergone a profound transition over the past decade.

Changes in capital financial markets

The first major change of the past decade has involved the creation of a global capital market. In my opinion, this idea remains in the visionary stage. In fact, the configuration of the world's markets does little to substantiate the existence of a single global entity—quite the opposite.

The Anglo-Saxon markets (primarily the United States and the United Kingdom), for example, are characterized by large and easily identifiable institutional capital formations, by a split financial system (commercial banks/investment banks), by open disclosure and reporting requirements, by highly influential rating agencies and research analysts, by a broad acknowledgement of the rights of shareholders and by a general absence of central authority. Market participants tend to be opportunistic.

The Japanese market, although it has large institutional capital formations and a split financial system, maintains relatively closed disclosure and reporting policies, does little in the way of acknowledging the rights of shareholders and, to a large measure, appears to be centrally orchestrated, if not managed. Ratings and research play a significantly less important role in Japan than they do in the United States or the United Kingdom.

The Continental European markets are once again different. The markets are dominated by single-entity universal banks, institutional capital formations are far fewer, and few of the institutions adhere to the strict disciplines common in the Anglo-Saxon markets. Disclosure and reporting requirements are lenient, rating agencies and analysts are just beginning to exert influence and shareholders have few rights. The influence of the central authorities runs the entire range, from dominant to non-existent. Market participants stress capital preservation.

Each of these three market groups has its own dynamic, its own series of investment principles, its own trading protocols and its own set of languages. Although the central banks governing these markets may consult each other on interest rate or monetary policy, the issuers, investors and intermediaries operate within the accepted practices of their own market.

Thus, the first major change is not really change at all. It none the less presents challenges to the sovereign issuer because, to gain complete market access, one still must contend with three distinct concepts of what a capital market is. In addition, in the past decade each of these major market groups has undergone its own transition on a regional basis. This transition has been most pronounced in the United States and the United Kingdom, where the influences of the institutional money management community are essentially reshaping market structure and redefining the historic roles of the financial intermediaries, most notably the investment banks.

In the United States, ERISA (Employee Retirement Income Security Act) funds have increased 79 per cent since 1980; mutual fund assets have grown 958 per cent over the past 10 years. In the United Kingdom, institutional assets under management have grown 182 per cent in the past decade. Insurance companies and trust institutions worldwide also sit atop vast and growing capital pools.

New means

If sovereigns are to develop as independent financial entities, they must tap into these capital pools, both in terms of equity, through privatization and debt/equity programmes, and of fixed income, through the issuance of government and agency bonds.

The question is how to do it? Whereas, several years ago, the backing of one or two major investment banks would enable an issuer to tap into considerable institutional capital, this is no longer the case because institutional investors are pursuing an increasingly sophisticated course in their approach to money management. Their greater size enables them to bring the analytic function in house. As a consequence, their historic reliance on the research supplied by investment banks is diminishing. The emphasis on internal equity and credit analysis has also gained impetus because the investment banks have done little to enhance their own credibility over the past several years. The junk bond crisis and collapse of Drexel have shaken investor confidence in investment banks and have brought the due diligence process closer to home.

Furthermore, the bond markets are becoming an institutional clubhouse. In the United States, over half of all senior debt is issued on a private placement basis. The private placement market is relatively restricted, with well-regarded credits enjoying relatively direct access to vast pools of capital and weaker credits often shut out of the market altogether, especially since the recent disruptions of the junk bond sector.

Where does this put the sovereign issuer? Sovereigns need to build direct links to the capital pools in the industrialized nations. They need to take their case directly to the market and work on reconstructing their image. Investment banks should be viewed as one of several media for market participation, rather than the single conduit. Negotiations that have historically taken place behind closed doors need to be brought out to centre stage and conducted in the broadest arena possible. This is particularly important for Central European countries because they have a valid opportunity to start afresh on the world market with a relatively clean slate. In a sense, many of these countries began building their present financial image only within the past year.

Countries seeking access to the capital markets have to view themselves more like large transnational corporations—entities like General Motors, Deutsche Bank, Toyota or General Electric. In 1989, these four entities alone drew $95 billion from the world's capital markets. They did it by interfacing with the market in the broadest context. Of course, investment banks played a crucial role in their capital-raising activities, but the direct links these entities have built with the world's institutions were the decisive factor in their ability to draw funds in such large volume.

This is the approach many sovereigns will have to take if they are to integrate in the world financial community.

Chapter 11

REINTRODUCING THE WESTERN FINANCIAL SYSTEM TO EAST-CENTRAL EUROPE: A CASE STUDY — POLAND

Witold S. Sulimirski*

The Yalta agreement of 1945 led to the imposition of an alien political and economic order on the countries of East-Central Europe. While it assured peace and growing prosperity for the West, the 100 million people of East-Central Europe paid a tremendous price. The 45 years of Soviet-dominated totalitarianism failed to break the spirit of the people or their aspirations for the right to choose and their cultural and ethnic identities. What it succeeded in doing, however, was to destroy the economies of the countries of the region and prevent them from realizing their potential.

The questions before us are the following. Will those countries be able to meet the challenges before them? Will the leadership, management and workers be able to adjust to the harsh realities of competitive market economies? What are the prospects for their being integrated into the mainstream global financial markets? I will focus on Poland as a case study, but the general principles are applicable throughout the region.

*Chairman of Intercap Investments, Inc., New York; former Executive Vice-President, Irving Trust Co.

The people

Let me start with the people. The Communist system's one success story is that of education. The general level of education, particularly in Hungary, Czechoslovakia and Poland, has always been high, reflecting traditions emanating from the universities of Prague and Cracow, both of which were established in the fourteenth century. Despite communism's persistent policy of promoting teachers and professors who were ideologically sound in preference to those who were more capable, a highly professional and gifted educated class developed, so much so that the sluggish economies of those countries were unable to absorb them. As a result, thousands of doctors and engineers were permitted to work in the oil-producing countries of the Middle East and North Africa.

The crash industrialization programme of the post-Second World War era also produced a large pool of skilled workers. However, the poor pay and abysmal working conditions, as well as the minimum safety net provided by the socialist welfare system, demotivated them completely. Moreover, many of them are employed by antiquated smoke-stack industries and will thus require extensive retraining.

Can these large pools of talent be motivated to work hard and productively? Personal observation suggests that the answer is a resounding "yes", subject to two very important provisos—financial incentives and inspiring leadership. This judgement is borne out by the work East Europeans do when abroad or when working for private companies in their own countries, and even in the case of a handful of well-managed State enterprises.

Management

Leadership, or management, is therefore the key. The old system called for the Communist party to approve every managerial appointment or promotion. Only its members could be on the so-called *nomenklatura* list of those eligible for positions of responsibility. Some of the potentially ablest people were thus excluded. Even more damaging was the centralized command system itself. Initiative at the lower level was frowned upon, bosses ruled by fear, backed by the omnipresent inform-ers of the secret police. Contacts with Western managerial thought and development were virtually non-existent.

The sad results can be observed in everyday dealings with the bu-reaucracy. The basic principles of managing the process, managing time and managing people are absent. There is a lack of communication and feedback in relation to co-workers and outsiders. Even worse is the absence of any realization of how important communication is. A log-ically and neatly presented proposal is a rarity indeed. Feedback on a proposal made to them is even rarer. Permeating these problems is the reluctance to make decisions.

Superimposed on the problems of management and labour, of atti-tudes and poor practices, are layers of other impediments to the rein-troduction of market-driven economies. Among them are the totally distorted banking, accounting and tax systems, as well as an inadequate legal framework.

Banking practices

The problem as it relates to the Soviet Union was succinctly described in the 4 August 1990 issue of *The Economist*:

> "Banks look like Western commercial banks in that they take depos-its and lend on to companies. But they do not have independent lending policies. They have no way of assessing creditworthiness. Soviet accounting practices cannot hope to hint at the state of corpo-rate health. Nor can the commercial banks provide companies with the discipline of being refused new money: they are required to give failing firms credit on demand."

An identical situation prevailed throughout the Eastern bloc. Banks were, in effect, channels for credit distributed in accordance with plan. There was very little difference between "donations", or capital alloca-tions, and credit. Accounting had two principal objectives: to make sure that plans were being fulfilled and to make sure that there was no fraud. The bookkeeping, therefore, was meticulous. Yet, ideas of cost, of capital allocation, of management information systems, other than as relating to the plan, were virtually non-existent.

Enter the new governments. The first one, in Poland, just a little more than a year ago, was charged with the task of reintroducing a market and profit-driven economy, as well as private ownership of property and of the means of production. Hungary had started on that road while still under the old regime. On a more limited scale, Poland did, too, the others not at all. Even today, those countries including Czechoslovakia, have hardly moved.

Poland immediately chose the most dramatic path. I wish to focus on the reform programme's practical impact on the country's financial system, particularly as it relates to the challenge of re-Westernizing and bringing it back fully into the international arena.

Impact of the reform programme
on the financial system

Throughout the 45 years of Communist rule, the banking system maintained contact with its Western counterparts in order to assure credit and the flow of payments for goods and services. International standards were generally maintained, for example, through adherence to the uniform customs of the International Chamber of Commerce. There has also been extensive personal contact: many East European bankers were trained in Western Europe and the United States.

International financial contacts remained active in other areas as well. On the one side, there have been, since the early 1980s, the frustrating rescheduling discussions with the Club of Paris and the Club of London. On the other, more productive side, Poland rejoined and established excellent relations with the International Monetary Fund and the World Bank, as well as with the International Finance Corporation.

Domestic banking operations, however, remained pretty isolated. Specialized banks took care of such sectors as agriculture and construction, dispensing credit in accordance with directives. Savings banks tapped the money that people were unable to spend for lack of supply.

In the case of Poland, blessed with a diaspora 10–15 million strong, citizens were permitted to maintain hard-currency accounts which now exceed $4 billion. It is estimated that at least an equal amount can be found under mattresses.

The Polish banking system had a head start along the road of reform. In 1988, the National Bank, which until that time had performed the dual role of a central and commercial bank, spun off 10 of its branches in the provinces into regional banks. While the decentralization brought some benefits, the regional banks continued to adhere to the same policies of credit allocation. Moreover, mechanisms normal to a multi-bank system, such as an interbank money market and a clearing-house, were not put in place. As a result, payments within the country were, and still are, subject to great delays. During the period of hyperinflation which Poland suffered in 1989, these delays were extremely costly to the payees. By the time they received payment, the purchasing value of the money might have halved.

Three pieces of legislation enacted by the old regime in 1989 provided the foundation for a modern banking system and adopted the continental model of a universal bank. This body of law further defined the specific role of the National Bank as the country's central bank and permitted the establishment of private banks, including banks entirely foreign owned. So far, 30 new banks have been authorized, mostly small community banks and including one with foreign capital.

The current stabilization programme in Poland relies heavily on the National Bank to curtail the money supply and stifle demand by way of high interest rates. The rapid throttling of inflation would suggest that the National Bank has been successful in its new role. The Bank is also taking measures to make the commercial banking system more efficient. The creation of a clearing-house, an interbank money market, a telecommunications system, more effective bank oversight, training centres for bankers, a chart of accounts recommended by the European Economic Community and minimum capital requirements recommended by the Bank for International Settlements are all under study or in the process of development. As importantly, during a meeting held at the National

Bank in July 1990, the chief executives of all the commercial banks were urged to participate actively in the process of privatization and to forge closer working ties with the international financial community.

The process of privatization will no doubt play an important role in developing the country's financial system and helping create a capital market. The privatization law, though not ideal in that the procedures it calls for are overly onerous, will finally be in place shortly. It has already stimulated considerable activity on the part of foreign investment and merchant banks, particularly from the United Kingdom, five of which have won mandates to privatize State-owned companies. Major international accounting firms have also arrived, some of them establishing links with existing Polish consulting firms. Investment banking activities are about to be commenced by the Warsaw office of the United States Government's Polish-American Enterprise Fund, and a subsidiary of Bankers Trust Company is expected to commence operations before year-end. The International Finance Corporation is working on a broadly empowered joint venture bank linking a couple of Polish Government banks with Western institutions.

Poland has dusted off one of Europe's best commercial codes, enacted in 1934 and based largely on the Swiss commercial code. New legislation, however, is required, particularly in the tax area.

A working group of Poles and foreign experts at the Ministry of Finance is preparing the groundwork for a stock market, as well as for other components of a capital market, including a regulatory body. The need for the latter is apparent, as enterprising entrepreneurs are already launching issues of questionable integrity. A debt-equity swap policy is under study. The Polish-American Congress in Chicago, an umbrella organization for Polish-Americans, is working on an issue of Polish State bonds, while several investment houses are prepared to launch "Poland funds" at short notice.

The Polish foreign investment law is relatively attractive, allowing complete foreign ownership of companies. Dividend repatriation rules have also been liberalized, and the success of the internal convertibility of the Polish currency, the zloty, bodes well for future capital mobility.

From what has been described above, the general prerequisites for Poland to become fully integrated into the world's financial markets appear to be falling into place. And yet, one can discern a certain ambivalence on the part of the Western investor, and even on the part of the average Pole. These question marks fall into three broad categories.

First, there is the concern that the plan of Finance Minister Balcerowicz has been overly ambitious and that it will collapse under the weight of rising internal political and social problems. Henry Kissinger, for instance, recently advised potential investors to wait things out for a few months. My personal view is that a shakedown period is fully consistent with the advent of democracy and that the general direction of change is irreversible at this time. There will, however, be personality clashes, differences of emphasis and modifications of individual programmes. Last year's prophets of doom were proven wrong, and, hopefully, so will today's. As a corollary to this uncertainty, there is doubt as to Poland's capacity to absorb capital. I am confident that, as described in this paper, the necessary financial and legal structure is in the making. It will assure that productive use can be made of the increasing inflow of official and private funds.

The second major cloud is the $40 billion debt overhang. This continues to brand Poland as a poor risk and is keeping away the major international banks, the key providers of crucial working capital. As Jeffrey Sachs said, in an article in the Summer 1990 issue of *Foreign Affairs*: "Poland's most fundamental financial need is for a deep and permanent reduction of its external debt burden. Otherwise, the debt burden will remain a profound barrier to economic development." While the prospects for a negotiated reduction of commercial bank debts under the Brady Plan are good, there appears to be no movement towards a reduction of the much larger government-to-government debt. The latter must become a priority for Finance Minister Balcerowicz.

The third area of latent concern relates to Polish populist attitudes towards foreign capital. Years of Communist propaganda about "foreign capitalist blood suckers" have left their mark, as has the much more prevalent fear of domination by German capital. One can also hear occasional nationalist voices harking back to pre-war ideas of economic self-sufficiency. Isolated as Poles have been, they are unaware of the tremendous international mobility of capital, of the benefits cross-border investments have brought and of the general interdependency of the world's economies. They are definitely unaware of the fact that at the present time, the international economy is driven more by investment than by trade. The Polish Government is endeavouring to foster understanding of these dynamics, yet the foreign investor needs to be aware of the sensitivities involved.

Conclusions

Despite its painful legacy, Poland is overcoming most of the obstacles that might prevent it from benefiting fully from international capital flows. The institutional framework either exists or is being put in place. The few internal and external barriers that remain will recede as political maturity grows. At the same time, foreign Governments and investors must realize that the success of the Polish experiment is crucial to the success of the change taking place throughout East-Central Europe and the Soviet Union. Over the past 10 years, these countries have closely followed developments in Poland. They will draw their lesson from any failure. It behoves us to assure that there will be success.

Chapter 12

THE ROLE OF
THE INTERNATIONAL
MONETARY FUND
IN GLOBALIZED
FINANCIAL MARKETS:
SOME IMPLICATIONS

Azizali F. Mohammed*

The globalization of financial markets in recent years has changed the international system in significant ways and, hence, has implications for the International Monetary Fund (IMF) as the central monetary institution of that system. It is useful to remind ourselves, however, that the process of integration is far from complete. While there is already great freedom of capital movements between the major industrial countries, and progress can be expected to intensify as the remaining institutional barriers disappear, particularly in Western Europe, two important groups of countries remain more or less outside the international financial circuits: the group of Eastern European countries that have recently started these systemic reforms, an essential element for the success of which will be a closer linking of their economies with the global trading and financial networks; and many, but by no means all, developing countries, although we can expect gradual progress by more of these countries to a stage where they can participate in, and benefit from, the globalized financial markets.

*Director, External Relations Department, International Monetary Fund.

Implications of globalization

Turning to the consequences of the greater integration of financial markets, there are both advantages and risks—advantages, obviously, in that there have been efficiency gains, better intermediation of capital and greater diversification of portfolios, but risks, also, because the closer interlinking has made transmission of shocks across markets more rapid and, at times, more forceful, and these shocks are potentially destabilizing. There are clearly trade-offs here between greater macro-efficiency and macro-stability (or rather instability) that will need to be addressed both at the country level and for policy coordination between countries.

Both are of interest to the IMF in its daily work. As regards the policies of individual countries, there is surely a higher premium to be placed than before on sound policies, or policies that are regarded by markets as being sound. Markets may be expected to react sharply and quickly, for example, if there is a consensus that a particular country has relaxed its monetary policy in a way that can be expected to lead to a financial deterioration—an acceleration in inflation or an imminent depreciation—and so affect its creditworthiness. In other words, the punishment for lax policies comes about more quickly with the greater scope for capital movements. This is especially pertinent for developing countries that must rely on private investors, both foreign and domestic. Moreover, the discipline of the markets does not apply in a particularly smooth or steady fashion; it can be quite abrupt, as so many countries learned at the outbreak of the debt crisis.

This does not mean that the traditional types of macroeconomic policies—fiscal and monetary—are less effective, but the evidence from the main industrial countries does appear to indicate that policy makers find their job more complicated because they must make allowances for the manner in which markets will perceive their policies and must deal with such perceptions if they find them to be either excessively sanguine or unreasonably dismissive. Moreover, the definition of monetary aggregates has tended to blur, forcing a shift from rule-based monetary policy to a more judgmental approach that provides less of a nominal anchor for expectations. The same type of blurring affects balance-of-payments concepts. It was conventional to focus on the current account and to apply policy instruments such as the exchange rate to treat imbalances in it. With capital movements now capable of swamping trade or service flows in magnitudes that can be a multiple of their transaction values, policy instruments must deal with capital flows in their own right, rather than simply as "financing" constraints on the current account.

Policy coordination

Turning to international policy coordination, it is notable that the greater integration of financial markets has occurred over a period when the major industrial countries were moving gradually towards a more intensive system of policy coordination, with discussions between policy makers occurring in various forums—the Group of Seven major industrialized nations, the Fund's Interim Committee and elsewhere. There is certainly a greater awareness now of the implications for others of policy actions by any one of the major countries, and there is a type of peer pressure among them to act in ways that are not damaging to others. Clearly, the multilateral surveillance process, in which the IMF participates, is evolving in a pragmatic manner, spurred by the knowledge that markets react quickly to perceived discordance within or among the policy-making circles of the principal capital market countries.

In addition to the coordination of macro-policies, there are important questions to be raised about international cooperation in policing the movements of funds as a result of the globalization of markets and the greater scope for sudden movements of funds between countries. We have seen at the national level—in the United States, for example—how deregulation of the thrifts gave rise to conditions in which imprudent actions led to the crisis of the savings and loan institutions. Fortunately, we do not yet have an exact analogy at the international level, but we should be thinking about how to forestall the potential damage or to cope with the heightened risks that are inherent in a deregulated system. There would not be much support for any effort to reintroduce a highly regulated system—and, in any case, it would be difficult to put the genie back in the bottle! But we have seen an increase in the phenomenon of "regulatory arbitrage"—of funds being moved to the least regulated markets.

We will perhaps have to revisit the concept of deregulation, with a view to seeing whether it is possible to combine the advantages of deregulation—the freedom that allows more efficient intermediation of global savings—with maintenance of adequate minimum capital requirements, for example, and an effective system of prudential supervision that reduces the scope for abuse and the risks of systemic shocks.

This is a large topic but one that could usefully be debated, especially as to the role that could be played by intergovernmental organizations like the IMF to strengthen prudential regulation through improved statistics and technical assistance to supervisory authorities and in the course of consultations under the Fund's surveillance procedures.

Chapter 13

REGIONAL INTEGRATION IN EUROPE AND NORTH AMERICA: IMPLICATIONS FOR FOREIGN DIRECT INVESTMENT IN DEVELOPING COUNTRIES

Peter Hansen*

A s the world approaches the twenty first century, regional integration among developing countries is no longer a political aspiration; it has become an urgent economic imperative. Economic integration is proceeding rapidly in Europe, Asia and North America, so that the region, rather than the nation-state, is rapidly gaining pre-eminence as the key arena for policy-making in the political sphere and investment in the economic sphere.

In the European Community, the 1992 programme to complete the single market has been highly successful, both in terms of strengthening regional institutions and laying the foundations for a functioning economic and monetary union. The countries of Eastern Europe are

*Executive Director of the United Nations Centre on Transnational Corporations.

likely to become increasingly linked to the single market as they move towards market-based economies, and it has been the European Community, rather than individual countries, which is guiding policy in this area. In North America, the United States-Canada Free Trade Agreement is encouraging new foreign investment into and within the region and has boosted the efficiency of industry to the benefit of the region's consumers. In Asia, an alliance is emerging between Japan and the countries of the Pacific Rim and China, driven in large part by foreign direct investment flows. Developing countries are thus witnessing the rapid regionalization of their key trade and investment partners and are now facing the challenge of achieving progress in their own regional integration efforts.

Regionalization in the 1990s

Regionalization in the 1990s means more than free trade in goods, as it has tended to mean in the past: integration programmes are successfully removing restrictions on the movement of capital, persons and services between countries, vastly improving the potential for economic efficiency and higher living standards. Because of this, countries which remain outside regional alliances are likely to become increasingly marginalized, or de-linked, from the world economy in the next decade. If current trends continue, trade, investment, information and technology will flow increasingly within and between large regional markets, attracted by the magnet of buoyant demand and increasing returns to capital. Those countries which are left out of these global flows will face the prospect of stalled economic development and deteriorating living standards. Regional integration has become, in the 1990s, a key vehicle for gaining access to world markets and for attracting foreign investment, trade and technology.

Possible impact of regional economic integration on foreign direct investment

The theory of economic integration predicts that foreign direct investment both to and within a region will increase after two or more countries of the region integrate their economies by eliminating internal barriers to trade while leaving external trade barriers in place. Foreign direct investment inflows to the integrated region may rise for a number of reasons: (1) some firms "jump the tariff" to produce inside the region what they previously exported to it, once there is free trade within the bloc but tariffs remain against third-country goods ("defensive import-substituting investment"); (2) transnational corporations may increase foreign direct investment in the integrated area if the creation of a larger market leads to greater economic efficiency and lower costs of production ("rationalized investment"); (3) they may also step up their direct investment in the region to position themselves in markets which are newly opened or exhibit rapid growth as a result of the integration programme ("offensive import-substituting investment"). The first case refers primarily to the strategies of firms from third countries—that is, from outside the region—and represents a short-term, static (one-time) effect; the second and third cases refer to strategies of all firms, regional and extraregional, and the effects in these cases are dynamic (ongoing) and likely to occur over the medium to long term. In all cases, the integration effort triggers activities by transnational corporations which raise the aggregate level of foreign direct investment in the region. Regional economic integration is thus said to produce an investment creation effect. An important theoretical question is whether this "pull" effect of regional economic integration on foreign direct investment is at the expense of investment in other countries or regions.

The elimination of internal trade barriers is also likely to cause an investment diversion effect, or a realignment of investment capital among members of the trading bloc once protective barriers have been removed. If this occurs, foreign direct investment activity between countries in the region is likely to increase following integration, although the aggregate level of investment stock may remain the same: increased inflows of foreign direct investment in some countries may be offset by declines in others, as firms realign their organizational structures and value-adding activities to reflect a regional, rather than a national, market ("reorganization investment"). This may in turn attract still more inflows of foreign direct investment, if the associated rationalization of the region's industries and services allows for economies of scale, lower costs of production and/or higher returns to capital.

The impact of regional integration on foreign direct investment from the trading bloc is more ambiguous. Outflows of foreign direct investment may decline if goods and services from the region become more competitive because of integration, so that exporting rather than foreign direct investment becomes the preferred mode of penetrating overseas markets. Foreign direct investment is likely to rise, however, if the integration process leads to the increased transnationalization of the region's industries and services, so that firms will be more inclined to make overseas investments both for sourcing and for marketing reasons.

Numerous variables will determine the extent to which integration produces these effects on foreign direct investment. Among the most important are the level of economic development of the region and whether significant non-tariff trade barriers remain within the region after tariff barriers have been eliminated. In the first instance, if firms in developing countries are unable to specialize and achieve economies of scale—because of a poor regional infrastructure, for example, or a lack of investment capital—then the effects of regional economic integration on foreign direct investment are likely to be slight; also, developing countries may not attract new investment by transnational corporations after they integrate if the regional market is not sufficiently large or dynamic. Furthermore, the economies of developing countries are typically more competitive than complementary; their major markets are in the developed countries and integration thus has limited potential to expand market size. Everything else being equal, integrated groupings among developed countries are more likely to result in increased foreign direct investment than those among developing countries, since the former are generally better equipped with the technological and physical infrastructure, investment capital and consumer and industrial demand conditions, all of which are necessary to develop an integrated, dynamic regional economy.

If, after integration, significant non-tariff barriers remain among members, then it is less likely that a truly regional economy will emerge—whether among developed or developing countries—thus lessening the extent to which foreign investment in the region will rise in response to the removal of internal tariff barriers.

THE EUROPEAN COMMUNITY'S 1992 INTERNAL MARKET PROGRAMME

Past experience: institutional framework and impact on foreign direct investment

Early integration efforts in the European Community eliminated tariffs and quotas within the Community, to create a free trade area, and introduced a common external tariff, to create a customs union. The Treaty of Rome, which set out the objectives of the integration programme, was signed in 1957 and the creation of a common market was achieved by 1968, two years ahead of schedule. The European Free Trade Association (EFTA) was formed in the 1960s with the aim of increasing its members' bargaining position *vis-à-vis* the European Community; in the 1970s, free trade was extended to this group, making it the most preferred of the Community's trading partners. With regard to developing countries, the European Community granted preferences to a select group of countries which had previously benefited from trade advantages as colonies of the Community's members. These preferential arrangements subsequently evolved into the current Lomé Convention, which covers 66 ACP (African, Caribbean and Pacific) countries, and trade preference schemes for Mediterranean countries. Since 1971, the Community has also participated in the Generalized System of Preferences, which, while less generous than the former two programmes, allows developing countries in Asia and Latin America to benefit from trade concessions from the Community.

The data on early European integration, from 1957 up to the early 1980s, support the hypothesis that integration among developed countries boosts the level of foreign direct investment in the region by third countries; in the years following the formation of the Common Market and EFTA, United States transnational corporations were the main actors in this process. Furthermore, it appears that this concentration of investment capital in Europe was at the expense of developing countries. The share of United States foreign direct investment stock in Europe increased from 15 per cent in 1950 to 44 per cent in 1980, while the developing countries' share declined from 50 per cent to 25 per cent over the same period. Flow data paint a similar picture: in the period from 1950 to 1955, Europe accounted for 15 per cent of cumulated outflows of United States foreign direct investment; in the period 1961–1967, this share rose to 39 per cent, representing an increase of 225 per cent, against only 120 per cent for all countries and 67 per cent for developing countries.

Further evidence that European integration had a pull effect on inwards foreign direct investment is provided by the experiences of Spain and Portugal, which joined the Common Market in 1986: inflows of foreign direct investment grew by 121 per cent in Spain and 103 per cent in Portugal after they joined the Common Market, against growth rates of 51 and 37 per cent, respectively, in previous years. While joining the Common Market was a key variable in triggering this remarkable increase, low labour costs, favourable economic policies and buoyant economic conditions in Spain and Portugal were underlying reasons for increased investor interest in those countries. At the same time as they joined, United States foreign direct investment in North African countries dropped precipitously.

Institutional arrangements for 1992 and their expected effects

Although tariffs and quotas within the European Community have been eliminated, the regional economy has remained fragmented because of the persistence of high non-tariff barriers: the European

Commission has estimated that non-tariff barriers currently impose costs on Community industry of between $136 billion and $207 billion, roughly 5 per cent of the European Community's total GDP. The most significant barriers are closed public-procurement markets, differing technical, health and safety standards, and customs formalities at frontier posts. In many manufacturing industries, non-tariff barriers greatly reduce the potential for intraregional trade and investment. In the area of services, differing regulatory regimes often block cross-border market entry altogether.

The 1992 programme is an attempt to realize the ultimate goal of the 1957 Treaty of Rome: the creation of a single, integrated, internal market free of restrictions on the movement of goods, services, capital and persons. Impetus for the programme, proposed in 1985, was in part motivated by the fact that many firms in the Community, particularly in high-technology industries, have progressively lost ground to their American and Japanese competitors, not only in extraregional markets but in the Community itself. Micro-electronics, electrical equipment, office automation and information technology are examples of industries in which European Community firms, including large transnational corporations, have failed to keep pace with competition from the United States and Japan, both in terms of output and of ability to innovate.

The 1992 programme is intended to address these issues; it is hoped that the cost savings from regional harmonization, coupled with the opening up of national markets, including markets for corporate assets, to more intraregional competition, as well as cooperation, will improve the competitive position of European companies, particularly in high growth, technologically advanced businesses such as micro-electronics and telecommunications.

The prospect of a single market has resulted in an unprecedented wave of business activity in the European Community, as companies restructure to position themselves for 1992. This activity in the corporate sector, as well as unusually rapid decision-making by the European

Commission and the European Council, has given the programme a momentum and success rate far beyond expectations: by September 1989, over half of the 279 directives of the 1992 programme had been adopted by the Council.

Flows of foreign direct investment

Recent trends that show Europe to be attracting a substantial share of worldwide flows of foreign direct investment—almost 28 per cent in the period 1981–1987—appear to have continued in 1988 and 1989. This trend is projected to increase into the immediate future, as demonstrated by the capital expenditure plans of United States transnational corporations. A June 1989 survey showed that they planned to invest $23 billion in their European Community affiliates in 1990, an increase of more than 60 per cent from the 1986 expenditure level; in the rest of the world, planned capital expenditures increased by only 46 per cent over the same four-year period.

Within the Community, the pace of cross-border mergers and acquisitions has risen markedly in the past few years. In 1984 there were 155 mergers and acquisitions in the European Community involving the Community's top 1,000 firms; by 1988, that number had more than tripled to reach nearly 500. A striking trend is the growing predominance of cross-border mergers and acquisitions currently being made in the European Community—deals between firms from different Community countries or between a Community firm and a third-country firm. In 1988, 20 per cent of all mergers and acquisitions in the Community were cross-border deals, but among the Community's top 1,000 companies, cross-border deals represented over 40 per cent of the total, a 10 per cent jump from the previous year. The data indicate that while the greatest number of mergers and acquisitions are domestic, in terms of value, most corporate assets in Europe are being traded across, rather than within, national borders. These trends are likely to result in increased transnationalization of Western European manufacturing and service industries.

Implications of the 1992 programme for developing countries

The single market programme of the European Community poses three major challenges to developing countries: maintaining Community markets for their exports; maintaining current levels of inwards foreign direct investment by transnational corporations; and attracting future inflows of foreign direct investment in the face of rapidly expanding investment opportunities in both Western and Eastern Europe.

Since the Community has yet to formulate a clear external trade policy, it is unsure whether goods imported from third countries, including developing countries, will be granted the same, less or greater access to Community markets than they currently enjoy. It is possible that raw materials, components and final goods manufactured in third countries may not be granted barrier-free access to Community markets, cutting into direct exports from developing countries. Firms from developing countries may be obliged to invest directly in the Community if they wish to maintain their position in markets previously served through exporting.

Local content requirements, rules of origin and the harmonization of technical standards are matters of policy which may be cited by the Community to erect barriers against third-party goods. These measures are intended to protect Community firms from low-cost imports, to attract foreign direct investment and to encourage subcontracting from Community firms rather than from third-country suppliers. However, even if such trade barriers are put in place, exports from developing countries may rise in the long-term if the economic effects projected to occur from the 1992 programme change the structure of European production: if Community firms shift out of industries which compete directly with exports from developing countries, such as clothing, steel and low-technology manufactured goods and into more skilled and technology-intensive industries, then exports from developing countries could rise to meet demand in markets which were previously served by European firms.

Maintaining current levels of inwards foreign direct investment

Recent decisions by the Community concerning trade in photocopiers and integrated circuits indicate that in the short term it may opt for external restrictions in certain sensitive areas. In both cases, penalties were imposed on the suppliers, which were from third countries, with the aim of encouraging the performance within the Community of the most substantial or technology-intensive aspect of production.

These policy measures, though largely trade-related, could have a direct effect on foreign direct investment in developing countries. Many transnational corporations invest in developing countries or sub-contract from developing country firms in order to export components and final goods to third countries, taking advantage of low production costs for labour-intensive operations. Stringent local content requirements and rules of origin contained in the 1992 programme are likely to encourage transnational corporations wishing to gain access to Western European markets to invest directly in the Community rather than in developing countries for export to the Community and to utilize European subcontractors, even though the latter may be more costly than those in developing countries. Also, the harmonization of European technical standards could mean that transnational corporations will be more inclined to locate research and development activities in the Community; thus, technology transfer to developing countries may also be threatened by the 1992 programme.

Since transnational corporations are currently taking measures in anticipation of possible restrictions against third countries in the 1992 programme, foreign direct investment in developing countries is likely to have already been adversely affected by European integration, even though the Community has not yet formulated its external policy. For instance, Intel, one of the world's leading manufacturers of computer chips, with substantial interests in developing countries, has recently invested $400 million in the European Community, a decision directly motivated by the above-mentioned local content policy on integrated circuits. In another example, the head of Sony in Europe, speaking about his company's plan to invest several hundred million dollars in Europe, was quoted in the 2 October 1989 issue of *Financial Times* as saying: "If we followed just the economics of manufacturing, we'd ship the lot from South-East Asia." At best, these new investments represent an opportunity cost to developing countries in terms of investment flows being diverted to Europe; at worst, there may be a real decline in current levels of foreign direct investment stock if transnational corporations move current capacity from developing countries to the European Community in order to assure market access after 1992.

Attracting future inflows of foreign direct investment

Future flows of foreign direct investment to developing countries are likely to be affected by shifting patterns of economic growth induced by the 1992 programme; these effects may have both positive and negative consequences.

Rapid growth of profitable opportunities in Europe triggered by the larger market may result in lessened future flows of foreign direct investment to developing countries, as the attractiveness of investment in Europe increases in relation to developing countries. Countering this possible decline are two factors which may lead to increased foreign direct investment in developing countries. As competition in the Community increases, cost reduction is likely to become a more important strategic objective for transnational corporations operating in the Community. They may thus increase foreign direct investment in developing countries, particularly in those which have special trading relationships with the European Community, such as the Mediterranean countries and exporters benefiting from the Generalized System of Preferences.

Secondly, in the long run the unification programme should strengthen the competitive position of transnational corporations from the European Community in global markets. This, too, may lead to increased foreign direct investment in developing countries, as transnational corporations from the European Community increase their worldwide sourcing and marketing activities.

Recent events in Eastern Europe could also influence the impact of the single market on investment in developing countries. If the liberalization of the socialist bloc economies leads to their economic growth and increased participation in international trade and investment, then they may invest more in developing countries. However, in the short and medium term, recent developments in Eastern Europe are likely to lead to a diversion of foreign direct investment from developing countries. Many transnational corporations are now actively looking at investment opportunities in the newly-opened economies of Eastern Europe, mostly with the aim of exporting low-market goods and services to Western Europe. Examples include General Electric's recent investment of $150 million in a factory in Hungary as part of its strategic plan for 1992. A statement, quoted in the 27 November 1989 issue of *Business Week*, by the chairman of Saint-Gobain, one of France's largest transnational corporations, is instructive in its implications about the impact of events in Eastern Europe on developing countries: "Everyone is talking about the business opportunities in South-East Asia. What luck to have the same opportunities suddenly open on our doorstep." Should the economies of Eastern Europe remain open to foreign direct investment and should they be granted some form of duty-free access to Community markets, then it is likely that they will displace some developing countries as attractive locations for direct investment by transnational corporations, both for export-oriented investment in the medium term and import-substituting investment in the long term.

Given the high degree of uncertainty surrounding the Community's external policy, some firms in developing countries which previously exported to the Community markets are investing directly in the Community in order to assure market access after 1992. Some developing country governments are implementing programmes to facilitate these investments and to ensure as much as possible that the Community retains an external policy which is as open as possible.

Brazilian companies, for instance, have responded to the trade and investment implications of 1992 by increasing investment in the Community, to the extent that Brazil is now the fourth largest investor in

Portugal. In India, several engineering companies are planning links with European firms, and a proposal has been made to the Finance Ministry to grant foreign exchange to Indian companies which establish European operations. Firms from the Republic of Korea are actively planning for joint ventures and mergers with European companies.

Many of these moves are being made in anticipation of future decisions by the European Community. Since the latter has not yet formulated its harmonized external policy, which is likely to be among the most difficult tasks in the unification programme, it is currently an auspicious time for governments in developing countries to participate in the debate. By strengthening their own regional integration efforts, developing countries will be in a better position to ensure that they will not be denied fair and equal access to the economic benefits which are sure to be created by the single market programme in 1992.

THE CANADA-UNITED STATES FREE TRADE AGREEMENT

The United States-Canada Free Trade Agreement, which was signed in January 1989, is notable for being the first trade agreement to explicitly liberalize foreign direct investment and trade in services between its signatories. Foreign direct investment will be affected by the Agreement in two ways: through the new rules on investment, described below and through the removal of tariffs and non-tariff barriers, as transnational corporations, which account for about 70 per cent of merchandise trade flows between the two countries, revise their cross-border investment strategies in response to free trade.

The Agreement liberalizes foreign direct investment in a number of ways, the most important of which is the establishment of the principle of national treatment between the United States and Canada, so that, while each country's national policies regarding investment will remain in effect, the other party's firms cannot be treated less favourably than domestic firms with respect to the establishment, acquisition and operations of a business. In addition, neither Government will be allowed to impose performance requirements on firms from the other country and the Agreement raises the asset threshold level at which Canada will review any new acquisitions by American firms. Canada has also waived the right to review indirect American acquisitions, that is, purchases of firms that were previously foreign-owned.

The principle of national treatment has been extended to include 64 commercial services. Trade in services is further liberalized by facilitating border crossing of personnel and by the stipulation that neither country may require service firms of the other to establish a business in order to provide a service, if doing so violates the national treatment principle.

The Agreement, while broad in scope, does not represent a major shift in Canada-United States economic relations: already about 70 per cent of bilateral trade is duty free. In the area of foreign direct investment, the Canadian acquisition review process has not represented a significant barrier to foreign direct investment by the United States in Canada in recent years. Both countries are allowed to maintain their respective domestic regulatory policies; in finance, for example, while national treatment means that American banks will be able to offer a full range of financial services in Canada, Canadian banks in the United States will be restricted from this practice by Glass-Steagall laws.

The provisions covering services secure rather than establish free trade in services, which are already traded relatively freely between the two countries. The real significance of the agreement on services lies in the fact that it sets a precedent for future multilateral trade negotiations.

Canadian manufacturing industries which are likely to be most affected by the Agreement following the removal of trade barriers include petrochemicals, metal alloys, clothing and several resource-based products, all of which faced high or escalating tariffs in the United States. The United States will primarily benefit from national treatment and larger public procurement markets, particularly in advertising and other commercial services.

Impact on foreign direct investment within and to the region

Foreign direct investment plays a key role in the trade flows between the two countries, and thus any agreement which influences their trading relationship is also an investment policy instrument. In fact, foreign direct investment plays a larger role than bilateral trade in the commercial relationship between the two countries: in 1987, sales resulting from foreign direct investment (sales of United States affiliates in Canada, plus the sales of Canadian affiliates in the United States) exceeded sales resulting from bilateral trade (imports plus exports) by 69 per cent. Canada is the largest single host country of United States foreign direct investment, which totalled $61.2 billion in 1988, about 70 per cent of total foreign direct investment in Canada. Canadian foreign direct investment stock in the United States totalled $27.4 billion in 1988; though still large, the gap between the investment positions of the two countries has been steadily narrowing since 1975.

Data on capital investment plans by United States affiliates indicate that the Free Trade Agreement had an initial positive influence on northbound foreign direct investment flows at least in the manufacturing sector.

In a survey taken in June 1988, before ratification of the Free Trade Agreement, United States transnational corporations reported plans to decrease capital expenditures in their Canadian manufacturing affiliates by 5.4 per cent. Six months later, in December 1988, when ratification of the Agreement appeared more certain, these plans were revised upwards to show a planned increase of 11 per cent for 1989, 1 per cent more than the planned revision for all countries. In June 1989, when the Free Trade Agreement had been in effect for six months, plans were further revised upwards to show a 20 per cent increase in planned 1989 expenditures, more than twice the planned increase for all countries.

In the case of Canadian foreign direct investment in the United States, it is expected that the Free Trade Agreement will have a net effect of slowing down its rate of growth, which has averaged 20 per cent a year over the period 1977–1987. A major motive for Canadian transnational corporations to invest in the United States has been market access in the face of rising United States protectionism—"defensive import-substituting investment". In so far as the Free Trade Agreement assures such access, there is likely to be a slow-down of Canadian foreign direct investment in the United States.

Perhaps the most significant long-term impact of the Free Trade Agreement on foreign direct investment will be to increase investment in Canada from third countries. While the Canadian market is small—a population of only 26 million—many large markets in the United States can be profitably served from a Canadian base, given Canada's abundant natural resources, cheap energy, geographical proximity, excellent infrastructure and relatively inexpensive labour. Just as Japanese car manufacturers have chosen to locate production in Tennessee because of its central location and low labour costs, so will transnational corporations increase investment in Canada, now that they are assured of duty-free access to the United States market. The Hyundai Motor Company, for instance, assembles cars in Canada for the entire North American market. Although currently the share of foreign investment by third countries is low, it has been growing rapidly in the past few years: in 1988, Japan accounted for about 3 per cent of total foreign direct investment in Canada, but its 1980–1988 annual growth rate exceeded 22 per cent, the highest of any country.

The Free Trade Agreement has greatly increased the pace of mergers and acquisitions in Canada, as transnational corporations restructure and rationalize in order to adjust to the free trade environment. The total value of mergers and acquisitions in the first half of 1989—estimated at $Can 20 billion—was nearly as high as the value for the previous twelve months—$Can 24 billion; non-Canadian companies have been estimated to account for about one third of transactions in the past few years.

Notable examples of strategic reactions by transnational corporations to the Free Trade Agreement include Proctor & Gamble's decision to

integrate its four Canadian plants into its existing United States operations, as part of a plan to "forget about the border"—"reorganization
investment". As a result of the Free Trade Agreement, both Du Pont
and Dow Chemical are increasing investments in their Canadian
export-oriented operations—"rationalized investment". Where transnational corporations relied on tariff and non-tariff barriers to remain
competitive, divestment has been the response to free trade—"investment diversion": Gillette has closed down its razor and pen-making
facilities in Canada, and Whirlpool and Burlington also plan to cut
back on Canadian production, preferring to export to Canada from
United States plants.

Implications for developing countries

The Free Trade Agreement is likely to have the greatest impact on
foreign direct investment in developing countries in the automobile
sector. Several developing countries have established important links
with North American transnational corporations, supplying them with
parts and/or assembled vehicles. Although the Free Trade Agreement
leaves intact the Auto Pact, which liberalized United States-Canadian
automotive trade in 1965, it raises the effective local content requirement for duty-free treatment from 50 to 70 per cent. Thus, the Agreement not only encourages third-party car makers to invest directly in
North America rather than export to it, but also means that any new
investment in the North American car industry is likely to incorporate
less-developing country value added than if there had been no Agreement. In fact, Hyundai, which currently incorporates only about 25
per cent Canadian value added in its Canadian-made cars, plans to
increase this to the target of 50 per cent direct Canadian value added—
equivalent to about 70 per cent total value added—in order to meet the
requirements of the Free Trade Agreement.

This trend, however, is not expected to include the operations
of Ford, General Motors and Chrysler, which already surpass the
Agreement's content requirement and could, in fact, increase their

sourcing from developing countries without violating the terms of the Agreement.

The duty-free benefits of the Free Trade Agreement are extended only to goods and services originating in Canada or the United States; the rules of origin stipulate that products and services must undergo substantial transformation in North America and/or incorporate at least 50 per cent or more North American value added. These provisions were put into the Agreement to protect Canadian industry from imports from low-cost producers, and they have helped stimulate Mexico's interest in becoming a third member of the Free Trade Agreement.

Because of these stringent rules of origin, developing country exports may suffer a price disadvantage *vis-à-vis* the same goods produced in Canada for export to the United States. However, existing United States duty-free arrangements with developing countries and regions, such as the Generalized System of Preferences, will remain in place. Also, Canada's comparative advantage in natural resources processing and capital-intensive industry rather than in assembly-type light manufacturing means that Canada does not pose a significant threat to rationalized investment—that is, export-oriented investment in low-cost areas—by transnational corporations in developing countries.

In some sectors, transnational corporations from developing countries may find it necessary to replace exporting with foreign direct investment in North America ("import-substituting investment") once tariffs are removed between the United States and Canada but remain in place against selected products from third countries. For instance, in September 1989, the Gerdau group of Brazil purchased a Canadian steel mill for $52 million, thereby gaining access to state-of-the-art steelmaking technology while bypassing United States quotas on Brazilian steel. Both defensive and offensive import-substituting investment in Canada by transnational corporations from developing countries is likely to increase in response to the Free Trade Agreement, particularly in natural resources processing and the automotive industries.

VOLUME II
ECONOMIC CHANGE

VOLUME IV
CHANGES IN THE HUMAN DIMENSION OF DEVELOPMENT, ETHICS AND VALUES

UNDP DEVELOPMENT STUDY PROGRAMME

The Development Study Programme of the United Nations Development Programme (UNDP) was established by the Governing Council of UNDP in 1981, in order to:

- Promote a greater understanding of the issues concerning development and technical cooperation;

- Strengthen public and governmental support for development and technical cooperation;

- Generate new ideas and innovative solutions to the problems of development and technical cooperation;

- Mobilize additional resources for development and technical co-operation.

The activities of the UNDP Development Study Programme take different forms such as seminars, lectures and informal discussion groups. Participants at the various events held under the auspices of the Programme are drawn from among high-level national policy makers, government representatives, senior officials of the United Nations system, leaders of public and private enterprises and representatives of the media and academics.

The UNDP Development Study Programme is financed from voluntary contributions of Governments, as well as international public and private institutions and foundations. Contributions may include the provision of hosting facilities and collaboration in organizing joint seminars and meetings.

William H. Draper III is the Administrator of UNDP and Üner Kirdar is the Director of UNDP Development Study Programme.

UNDP Headquarters is at One UN Plaza, New York, New York, 10017

ABOUT THE EDITOR

Üner Kirdar is currently the Director of the UNDP Development Study Programme; he has been the Director of the Division of External Relations and Secretary to the Governing Council Secretariat of UNDP since 1980.

Born in Turkey on 1 January 1933, he graduated from the Faculty of Law, Istanbul, undertook post-graduate studies at the London School of Economics, and received his Ph.D. from Jesus College, University of Cambridge, England.

Dr. Kirdar has served the United Nations system in various capacities, such as Secretary of the Preparatory Committee and United Nations Conference on Human Settlements (1974–1976), Secretary of the Group of Experts on the Structure of the United Nations System (1975), and a Senior Officer for Inter-Agency Affairs in the Office of the United Nations Secretary-General (1972–1977).

He has been the main architect of the UNDP Development Study Programme and has organized several seminars, round-table meetings, lectures and discussion groups attended by high-level national and international policy makers.

He has also held senior positions in the Ministry of Foreign Affairs of Turkey, including Director for International Economic Organizations and Deputy Permanent Representative of Turkey to the United Nations Office at Geneva.

Dr. Kirdar is the author of the book *Structure of UN Economic Aid to Underdeveloped Countries*, Martinus Nijhoff, (1966; 1968). He is the co-editor and contributor to other books: *Human Development: The Neglected Dimension* (1986); *Human Development, Adjustment and Growth* (1987); *Managing Human Development* (1988); *Development for People* (1989); *Equality of Opportunity Within and Among Nations*, Praeger Publishers, (1977); "Human Resources Development: Challenge for the '80s", *Crisis of The '80s*, (1983); "Impact of IMF Conditionality on Human Conditions", *Adjustment with Growth* (1984); *The Lingering Debt Crisis* (1985). He has also contributed numerous articles to professional books and journals.